# heartwarmers

# heartwarmers

## *Award-winning Stories of Love, Courage, and Inspiration*

BY
AZRIELA JAFFE

Adams Media Corporation
Holbrook, Massachusetts

Published by
Adams Media Corporation
260 Center Street, Holbrook, MA 02343. U.S.A.

ISBN: 1-58062-308-5

Printed in Canada.

J I H G F E

**Library of Congress Cataloging-in-Publication Data**
Heartwarmers : award-winning stories of love, courage, and inspirations /
[compiled] by Azriela Jaffe.
p.      cm.
ISBN 1-58062-308-5
1. Conduct of life.  I. Jaffe, Azriela.
BJ1597.H43 2000
158.1'28—dc21
99-086413

This publication is designed to provide accurate and authoritative information with regard to the subject matter covered. It is sold with the understanding that the publisher is not engaged in rendering legal, accounting, or other professional advice. If legal advice or other expert assistance is required, the services of a competent professional person should be sought.
—From a *Declaration of Principles* jointly adopted by a Committee of the American Bar Association and a Committee of Publishers and Associations

Cover illustration by Dan Wiemer.

This book is available at quantity discounts for bulk purchases.
For information, call 1-800-872-5627.

**Visit our exciting Web site: www.adamsmedia.com**

# Foreword

I REMEMBER BACK WHEN I WAS A TEENAGER—IN THE 1960'S—WHEN THERE WAS A local radio show that aired every morning. It was just a 10 minute segment and was called "One Man's Scrapbook." It was produced and narrated by a well known local personality, Edward "Eddy Jo" Joseph. Now this is not the kind of show that teenagers listen to, however, it was so different and unusual I couldn't help it. In later years, I had the pleasure to get to know and admire Mr. Joseph, who is famous for his immense collection of poems, quips, and inspirational stories. In fact, he even put a collection of them together in a book titled after the name of his radio show. This "scrapbook" is a treasure trove of humorous and poignant verse for practically any occasion.

So the thought occurred to me—why not try to do the same thing on the Internet? Why not spread a little optimism over cyberspace with a scrapbook of stories that would provide an alternative to the depressing day-to-day news? Since I already worked at home and spent a lot of time online, this could be a great way to do something that might actually benefit a few folks, not to mention my own need to be around positive ideas and people!

I had no idea how to approach this. But I did know that Internet mailing lists existed. I was a subscriber to one of the joke mailing lists, having a joke emailed to me everyday. So, I thought, why not have a free email service that people could subscribe to that sent out short stories every day? Stories that would help people overcome their day-to-day stresses and help them look on the bright side. Why not start something that was a conduit for something positive and uplifting? It could be the new millennium's version of the "positive thinking" books.

On May 27, 1998, I sent out my first "Heartwarmer" to a few friends who I put on my mailing list. I wanted to get the word out to others and send out a press release announcing the service that was described as: "The free email service that provides you with daily messages filled with inspirational stories from people around the world who tell their true tales of strength, courage, hope, and the triumph of the human spirit." Within a couple of weeks, word spread and people were joining the list.

It's been a wild ride. The power of the Internet grabbed this concept and ran with it. Within a few months, there were tens of thousands of subscribers in over 100 countries throughout the world and, within a short time, we became an Internet community. We no longer have subscribers—today we have "members." We have message boards that allow our members to communicate with each other, and they can also get a free Web page they can construct for themselves in a matter of minutes, giving them their own little corner on the "net."

But more importantly, there is a discovery taking place. In the process of sending out over a million pieces of email to our members every month, we have discovered new talent out there. Opening our email is like being in a gold mine. We never know when another nugget will turn up—another amazing story by an unknown writer who wants to be part of the Heartwarmers' experience. You see, when I started Heartwarmers4u, I had no idea where the stories would come from. Fortunately, it turned out that there were dozens of writers out there—excellent writers—who had little or no opportunities for exposure and who jumped at the chance to contribute. I couldn't pay them, but I could give them something the mainstream publishing industry could never give them—instant gratification.

members in the far corners of the world. It's an incredible system that will change the way we receive and react to information. This provides a new way that like-minded people—people who truly care about one another—can use to feel connected. Despite political or geographic boundaries, we have become a family.

Since cavemen chiseled their first words to today's fast as the speed of light data transmissions—people have all wanted the same thing. Human nature will never change. We all want to be appreciated and loved, we need to feel that what we are doing is worth something, we need to have something to look forward to, and we need to know there is hope. Heartwarmers4u is just the latest way to offer those precious, timeless, and sometimes rare emotions. One hundred years from now, when people are communicating in ways we can't even fathom today, the stories found in this book will have exactly the same meaning and impact.

This book is a milestone. It's the first one that is compiled of stories that originally appeared on the Internet and have become literal turning points in the lives of many of our members. And we hope they will become a turning point in your life as well.

Welcome to the world of Heartwarmers4u—where the "human spirit always triumphs!"

Lee Simonson, Founder, Heartwarmers4u
email: lee@heartwarmers4u.com
web site: http://www.heartwarmers4u.com

Join the Heartwarmers online community!
It's easy and free. Just send an email to:
join@heartwarmers.com

You see, by including their email address with their stories, our members are able to directly and instantly communicate with the writers. It is not unusual for our writers to receive hundreds of emails after their stories appear—each telling the writer how much his or her story had meant and touched their lives. Many of our writers have already become legends on the Internet, with their stories becoming modern day classics.

What you see compiled in this book is just a fraction of the stories that have made a tremendous impact on the hearts and minds of countless people around the globe. Inspiring tales that got their start at Heartwarmers4u, but continue to wind their way around our shrinking world in seconds, via forwarded email.

The stories—all original—have been submitted by these writers whose imaginations were captured by the newest electronic medium. They constitute a new breed of "cyberauthors" who will blaze a trail for generations to come as the Internet becomes a fixture in our daily lives—the same as television did a generation ago and radio even before that.

The success of Heartwarmers4u is due to many people. Folks like Bruce Watkins and his son, Bob, and Bruce's partner, John Zeder, who do all our web design work. (I don't know HTML code from hieroglyphics.) Lynn Schaufelberger hands out our Web site awards and Cookie Hungerbuhler provides a wealth of information on our message board.

The book that you are holding right now is due solely to one person whose tenacity and determination could not, and would not, be denied. It was her idea and she saw this project through from start to finish. Azriela Jaffe, a fellow heartwarmer and e-zine publisher, contacted me about putting some of our stories in a book. As they say, the rest is history. Thank you, Az!

Every evening, late at night, when I use my mouse to click the "Send" button, a technological process begins and invisible electrons start jumping all over the place. Data starts flowing and packets of information are routed through switches. Within moments, our heartwarming message magically arrives in the mailboxes of our

# Introduction

BY AZRIELA JAFFE

WHEN LEE SIMONSON EMAILED ME AND ASKED ME IF I'D LIKE TO BEGIN RECEIVING his new electronic magazine, called Heartwarmers4u, I said, "SURE," not because I understood anything about the list, but just because Lee asked and I thought he was a cool guy. Lee and I have known each other for a few years, meeting when I interviewed him for my book, *Starting from No: Ten Strategies to Overcome Your Fear of Rejection and Succeed in Business.*

Frankly, I couldn't imagine any e-zine I would look forward to receiving every day. I already receive something like 300 emails a day, and this seemed as if it would be burdensome. But I didn't want to let Lee down, and there was something amusing about not rejecting the guy I had interviewed about how to handle rejection.

Hah! Turns out, what he offered was one of the greatest Internet gifts I've ever received.

I was quickly transformed from wondering if I'd enjoy the list, to considering it one of my favorites. It only got better and better, and the longer I was on the list, the more an idea jelled in my head. Why not assemble the best of the best, the heartwarmer stories that draw the most email responses and generate the strongest heartfelt responses from the tens of thousands of members of this online community, and put them into a book? Certainly, those who eagerly await their heartwarmers in the morning would appreciate a book of their favorite stories that they could purchase for themselves and their friends. And this would also be a way to spread the word to others who are not yet familiar with Heartwarmers4u.

I approached Lee with the idea of my editing and writing such a project, and in a quintessential Lee manner, he said, "Sure, go ahead." And so, we did.

Selecting and editing the stories for this book was an awesome task. I had the privilege of reading every heartwarmer story ever written—hundreds of them! Winnowing down so many great stories to about sixty stories was no easy job. And then, there was the editing.

At first I was leery—would the writers of these deeply personal stories allow me to offer my professional editing expertise? Would they be offended if I requested changes to their stories or suggested new ways to express their stories? After all, I was messing with their "babies"!

To the authors' credit, they responded with gratitude, joy, and complete cooperation, as we came together as partners to make their stories the best they could be. Instead of responding defensively, they were delighted that their stories were chosen as award-winning heartwarmers, and they were open to shaping them into final masterpieces.

I have only one problem with this book. My job as a writer and editor is now over, and I'm going to miss one of the most heartwarming experiences of my life. But that's okay. We hope there will be many heartwarmers books. Enjoy!

PS: If you aren't already a subscriber to Heartwarmers4u, treat yourself. Subscription info is found on page viii of the book.

# The Red Mahogany Piano

MANY YEARS AGO WHEN I WAS A YOUNG MAN IN MY TWENTIES, I WORKED as a salesman for a St. Louis piano company. We sold our pianos all over the state by advertising in small town newspapers. When we had received sufficient responses, we loaded our little trucks, drove to the area, and sold the pianos to those who had replied.

Every time we advertised in the cotton country of Southeast Missouri, we would receive a reply on a postcard that said, in effect, "Please bring me a new piano for my little granddaughter. It must be red mahogany. I can pay ten dollars a month with my egg money." The old lady scrawled all over the back of the postcard until she had filled it up. Then she turned it over to write on the front and even around the edges, leaving barely enough room for the address.

We could not sell a new piano for ten dollars a month. No finance company would carry a contract with payments that small. So, we ignored her postcards.

One day, however, I happened to be in the area calling on other replies and out of curiosity I decided to look up the old lady. I found pretty much what I had expected. She lived in a one-room share-cropper's cabin in the middle of a cotton field. The cabin had a dirt floor, and chickens roosted in the house. She obviously could not have qualified to purchase anything on credit. She had no car, no phone, no job. All she had was a roof over her head and not a very good one at that. I could see daylight through it in several places.

Her little granddaughter was about ten, barefoot, and wearing a feed-sack dress.

I explained to the woman that we weren't able to sell a new piano for ten dollars a month and that she should stop writing to us every time she saw our ad. I drove away feeling heartsick, but my advice had no effect. She continued to send us the same postcard every six weeks. She always asked for a new piano, red mahogany, please, and swore she would never miss a ten-dollar payment. It was gut-wrenching.

A few years later, I owned a piano company, and when I advertised in that area, her postcards started coming to me. For months, I ignored them. What else could I do?

Then one day when I was in the area, something came over me. I happened to have a red mahogany piano on my little truck. Despite knowing I was about to make a terrible business decision, I went to her cabin and told her I would carry the contract myself. I said she could pay me ten dollars a month with no interest and that would mean fifty-two payments. I took the new piano in the house and placed it where I thought the roof would be least likely to drip rain on it. I admonished her and the little girl to try to keep the chickens off it, and I left—certain I had just thrown away a new piano.

But the payments came in, all fifty-two of them, as agreed—sometimes with coins taped to a three-by-five-inch card in the envelope. It was incredible!

I put the incident out of my mind for twenty years.

Then one day I was in Memphis on other business, and after dinner at the Holiday Inn on the levee, I went into the lounge. As I sat at the bar sipping an after-dinner drink, I heard the most beautiful piano music behind me. I looked around and spotted a lovely young woman, playing a very nice grand piano.

Being a pianist of some ability myself, I was stunned by her virtuosity. I picked up my drink and moved to a table beside her, where I could listen and watch. She smiled at me, asked for requests, and when she took a break, she sat down at my table.

"Aren't you the man who sold my grandma a piano a long time ago?" she asked.

It didn't ring a bell, so I asked her to explain.

She started to tell me, and I suddenly remembered. My Lord, it was her! It was the little barefoot girl in the feed-sack dress!

She told me her name was Elise. Because her grandmother couldn't afford to pay for lessons, she had learned to play by listening to the radio.

She started to play in church, to which she and her grandmother walked over two miles to attend. She also played in school, and won many awards and a music scholarship. She married an attorney in Memphis, and he bought her the beautiful grand piano she was playing.

Something else entered my mind. "Elise," I said, "it's a little dark in here. What color is that piano?"

"It's red mahogany," she said, "Why?"

I couldn't speak. Did she understand the significance of the red mahogany? Was she aware of the unbelievable audacity of her grandmother, insisting on a red mahogany piano when no one in his right mind would have sold her a piano of any kind? I think not. Did she grasp, then, the marvelous accomplishment of the beautiful, terribly underprivileged child in the feed-sack dress? No, I'm sure she didn't understand that either.

But I did, and my throat tightened.

Finally, I found my voice. "I just wondered what color the piano was," I said. "I'm proud of you. If you'll excuse me, I have to go to my room."

I really did have to go to my room, because men don't like to cry in public.

—JOE EDWARDS

*Joe Edwards has spent most of his working life as a jazz pianist in Kansas City nightclubs. He's now retired but still plays wedding receptions in the Springfield, Missouri, area.*

# 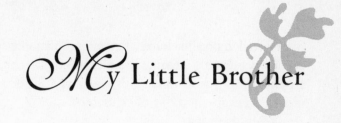My Little Brother

GROWING UP WITH A BROTHER WHO IS SEVEN YEARS OLDER THAN I AM was difficult.

I idolized Scott, and not being able to go to the places he did and to hang out with his friends hurt a lot. I always fell into the role of the dorky younger brother trying desperately to just fit in. All I ever wanted was to make him proud of me.

So, when Scott announced he was going to work the summer teaching mentally challenged kids and asked if I'd like to volunteer, I jumped at the chance to spend the time with him.

I was fourteen and the only volunteer in the program. Everyone else was twenty-one or older, and was either earning college credits in special education, like my brother, or trying to make a few bucks for the summer. The program included approximately thirty students, ranging in age from eight to twenty-one, with the majority being around my age. My exposure to the world of the mentally challenged was limited, and I was a bit taken aback on my first day.

Wheelchair after wheelchair rolled off the bus, each with its own special passenger, wearing a smile brighter than the sun in summer. Parents dropped off other kids, each one filled with the same excitement I'd felt my first day of school.

Then there was Mikey.

Mikey was nine years old, tall, thin, and severely emotionally disturbed. He stood alone in the corner, swaying back and forth, afraid. It seemed as if he was invisible to all the other students and counselors. I walked over to him and reached out my hand, and he began to scream. I remember the look of embarrassment in my brother's eyes. I wanted to crawl under a rock and just quit. I backed away and tended to the other students.

Every morning when Mikey's mother dropped him off, he went to the same corner, where he spent most of his day alone. Even other students avoided him, not wanting to provoke the screaming or tantrums he would throw.

Every afternoon the counselors asked their students to pair off for different activities. Mikey would remain in the corner, watching. Feeling more comfortable after a few days, I approached the director and asked her about Mikey. She explained he had been coming to the program for a few years, always spending his days just as he was then. No one had the time needed to spend with him. I asked if I could work with him. She didn't respond at first, and I could see the whole "You're only fourteen years old! What can you do?" look in her eyes.

"Sure, go ahead. What could it hurt?" she finally replied.

So each morning I'd wait for Mikey to arrive. When he walked over to his corner, I tagged right along and then would stand or sit next to him for hours, not saying a word. He would scream, and everyone would look, but I just stared straight back at them, determined not to quit. This went on for two weeks. I knew all the counselors were talking about me to my brother. The summer was not unfolding as I had envisioned; I had hoped to strengthen the bond between my brother and me, not weaken it.

Then something happened that changed my life forever. I overslept one morning, and my brother had already taken off to work. I jumped on my bike and rushed to the school, embarrassed for oversleeping and worried I was in trouble.

I walked into the classroom, and the room went silent. "Oh no," I thought.

Then I heard someone clapping his hands. I shrugged it off as one of the students just expressing his excitement. Then someone else began clapping. Another happy student, I thought. No, it was one of the counselors. What was going on? Then it erupted. Everyone was clapping. Were they all reacting sarcastically to my being late?

At that moment, I locked eyes with my brother.

He was smiling at me and clapping the loudest of everyone. I just stood there, puzzled, until the program director approached me and explained it had to do with Mikey.

Apparently, when Mikey arrived that morning and couldn't find me, he went from table to table and counselor to counselor, asking, "Where's Paul? Where's Paul?"

The director informed me those were the first words Mikey had spoken in the past couple years of his life.

I didn't know what to say.

My eyes filled with tears. I looked over to Mikey in his corner. He was smiling, pointing to me, and saying, "Paul! Paul! Paul!"

I felt a hand on my shoulder. It was Scott. "This is my little brother," he kept reminding everyone with pride in his voice. It was then I began to cry.

—PAUL W. KLEINSCHMIDT

*The next year Paul was hired to be a counselor. Mikey's family moved out West, and Paul was saddened at the prospect of never seeing him again. The last day of the program, he received a postcard from California with the words "Hi Paul" in Mikey's barely legible handwriting.*

*Paul is now an adult and works in the advertising department of International Male, a men's clothing catalog company based in San Diego, California. He lives in San Diego with his partner, Darryl, and his dog, Scruf.*

*Paul's brother Scott has worked for seventeen years as a special education teacher in Oshkosh, Wisconsin. Married in 1982, he and his wife, Terry, have three sons—Bryan, David, and Travis.*

*Although Paul took a different career path, his love for teaching and the joy he experienced in helping others shaped his life and made him the person he is today. He and Scott remain close to this day.*

# Nightly Friends

GLADYSE AVERY RAN A THRIVING NURSERY FOR MANY YEARS. THE PRIDE of Sanford, Maine, Mrs. Avery always offered the hardiest tomato sets and the most beautiful roses. It was a sad day when her doctor advised the lonely widow of her oncoming blindness.

I'd taken care of her clocks for many years. Although they were common shelf clocks, Gladyse thought of them as her companions in the quiet evenings. When she could no longer make out the numbers on the dials, she asked me to remove the glass in each of her clocks. When I dropped by her home to deliver the last of the modified clocks, she touched its hands and said, "Fine, fine, thank you."

As usual, she invited me to a cup of tea. It was already dusk, and the tea was ready. So, I helped her put the cups and saucers on a serving tray. She brought the steaming teapot over to the table, and I guided her hand as she set it on the tray.

"Let's sit by the back door," she suggested. "It's stuffy in here, and we can sit out there and listen to the crickets."

Sound and touch were particularly important to Gladyse after losing her eyesight. I reflected upon my vocation as a clockmaker, pondering how I would continue my work if I had limited eyesight or lost the use of a hand.

On the way out the back door, she scooped up a handful of what looked like cat food and I carried the tea tray. Quite capable of navigating to the solitary white table in the middle of the tiny secluded back yard, she took her usual seat. I sat down beside her and reached over to serve tea.

In complete darkness, we listened to the sounds of her world. She identified crickets, bullfrogs, a passing motorist, the neighbor's barking dog, and the meow of Mrs. Blackwell's cat. She asked me to take her hand and to point it at the north star and the twinkling stars in the sky. At that point, I started to get misty-eyed, witnessing this woman, a friend to many, coping with her new challenge of blindness.

We sipped our tea in silent companionship for a few minutes.

Reaching into her pocket, she fingered a few of the dry nuggets of cat food. Making a "kissing" noise, she held her hand close to the ground. I could barely see the image of a cat sauntering toward her chair and nuzzling its nose in the palm of her hand. A second and then a third cat emerged from the darkness. As I watched her feed and pet her little friends, I smiled at her kindness.

As my eyes adjusted to the dark and my vision became clearer, I almost leaped out of my chair when I realized she was feeding a family of skunks!

Holding my seat, gritting my teeth, and hoping I wouldn't startle her little friends, I nervously took another sip of tea. Her conversation never wavered as she continued to feed and pat the domesticated skunks circling her ankles.

Then, as quickly and stealthily as they had emerged from the dark shadows of her back yard, they left.

I never revealed to her what I saw that night—it would have been wrong to alter her innocence. God bless Mrs. Avery.

—ERN GROVER

*Ern and Anneke Grover reside in the little community of Springvale, Maine. Ern is a busy clockmaker and a frequent contributor under the pen name Madison Caldwell to the local newspaper,* Maine Yarnin'. *His collection of colorful and humorous stories will be published in 2000 in a book titled* Country Yarnin'.

# Behind the Mirror

WHEN I WAS A LITTLE GIRL, WE LIVED IN NEW YORK CITY JUST DOWN THE block from my grandparents. Every evening my grandfather would go for his "constitutional," and in the summers I would join him.

One evening when Grandpa and I went for our walk, I asked how things were different when he was a little boy from then, in 1964. He told me about outhouses instead of flush toilets, horses instead of cars, letters instead of telephones, and candles instead of electric lights. While he told me all the wonderful things I had never thought of living without, my little mind wandered. Then I asked him, "Grandpa, what was the hardest thing you ever had to do in your life?"

Grandpa stopped walking, stared at the horizon, and said nothing for a minute or so. Then he knelt down, took my hands, and with tears in his eyes began to speak:

"When your mom and her brothers were little children, Grandma got very sick and in order to get well, she had to go to a place called a sanitarium for a long time. I had no one to take care of your mom and uncles while I worked, so they went to an orphanage. The nuns took care of them for me while I worked two and three jobs to get your Grandma well and everyone home again.

"The hardest thing I ever had to do was put them in there. I went every week to see them, but the nuns wouldn't let me talk to them or hold them. I watched the three of them play from behind a one-way mirror. I brought them sweets every week, hoping they knew it was from me. I would keep both hands on the glass for the entire thirty minutes I was allowed to watch them, hoping they would come and touch my hand.

"I went a whole year without touching my children. I missed them very much. But I know it was a harder year for them. I will never forgive myself for not making the nuns let me hold them. But they said it would do them more harm than good and that they would have even more trouble living there. So I listened."

I had never seen my Grandfather cry before. He held me close, and I told him I had the best Grandfather ever and I loved him.

Fifteen years went by, and I never talked about that one special walk with Grandpa. We continued our walks for years, until my family and grandparents moved to separate states.

After my grandmother passed away, my grandfather experienced memory lapses and what I believe were periods of depression. I begged my mother to invite Grandpa to come and live with us, but she refused.

I kept harping, "It is our duty as a family to figure out what is best for him."

In a fit of rage, she snapped, "Why? He never cared about what happened to us!"

I knew what she was talking about. "He has always cared about and loved you," I said.

My mother replied, "You don't know what you're talking about!"

"The hardest thing he ever did was put you, Uncles Eddie and Kevin in the orphanage."

"Who told you about that?" she asked.

My mother had never discussed her days there with us.

"Mom, he came every week to see the three of you. He used to watch you play from behind the one-way mirror. He brought you sweets every time he visited. He never missed a week. He hated not being able to hold you for that year!"

"You're lying! He was never there. No one ever came to see us."

"How would I know about the visits if he didn't tell me? How would I know about the treats he brought? He was there. He was always there. But the nuns wouldn't let him be in the room with you, because they said it would be too hard when he had to leave. Mom, Grandpa loves you, and he always has!"

Grandpa assumed that his children knew he was there behind the glass, but because they had not felt the warmth and strength of his arms, he thought they had forgotten his visits. Meanwhile, my mother and her brothers assumed Grandpa had never come to visit. Telling my mother the truth changed her relationship with Grandpa. She learned that her father had always loved her, and Grandpa came to live with us for the rest of his life.

—LAURA REILLY

*Laura continues to write stories about her family and spends a great deal of time researching her family genealogy. She is an advertising executive and lives in the New York City area.*

# A Second Father

MY BEST FRIEND'S FATHER DIED WHEN SHE WAS FIVE. IT WAS HARD ON HER family. Her brother, eight years her senior, began to watch over their mother and her.

Because of their father's death, her mother was forced to get a full-time job. Her brother took on many more responsibilities than was ever expected of him. Hand-in-hand, he'd walk his little sister to the bus stop. As they waited, he played games with her like their father had. He tried everything to make her happy.

When they arrived home from school, he would sit her down with three cookies and a glass of milk and help her with her homework until their mother arrived home from work. Afterward, he did the laundry, prepared dinner, and washed the dishes to make it easier on their mom.

One Saturday in June a few years after her dad died, my friend went shopping with her mother. When she stared at a rack of Father's Day cards, her mom felt compelled to comfort her, saying, "Honey, I know this is a hard time for you."

"No, Mom, that's not it! Why don't they have brother's day cards?"

She picked out a Father's Day card for her brother, and with tears in her eyes, presented it to him on Father's Day.

As he read it, tears welled up in his eyes as well, and the three of them hugged. Her mom's voice cracked as she said, "Son, if your father was here, he would be so proud of you. He raised such a good man, and you have done your best to fill his shoes. We love you. Thank you."

—MELISSA KNAPP

*This event happened almost twenty-three years ago. Her best friend, Melissa, and her brother remain very close; they live in the same area and are in regular contact with each other.*

# Just the Way You Are

WHEN I WAS TWENTY-FOUR YEARS OLD, I UNDERWENT SEVERAL OPERATIONS to remove parts of my ovaries and tubes damaged from a fibrous condition. While I was recovering in the hospital, the doctors decided to remove some fluid from my uterus and test it for cancer. It came back positive. The following day, I received a total hysterectomy/oophorectomy.

I was devastated. I had structured my whole life around one day having a big family, and not being able to bear children seemed like the worst thing that could have happened to me. I didn't consider how lucky I was that the doctors found the cancer in time to save me. I went into a deep depression and stayed there for a long while.

At the time I was living at home with my parents and my younger sister. One day, she came home and told us she was pregnant.

I could not bear the pain of knowing she would soon have a baby and I could never have one. She was unmarried, which I think probably made me feel worse. A succession of baby toys, baby clothes, and baby showers tortured me for nine months. I spent every evening alone in my room, crying and asking God what I had done that was so wrong. I never got an answer.

Well, the baby girl came and she was beautiful. But I never held her, at least when anyone was around. Late at night I would go downstairs and sit in the rocker, rocking her and singing to her.

My father loved her. A big, stern Marine, he would soften like butter when he held Monica Sue. It hurt me so much to think I could never give him a grandchild. I continued living in my depression.

One night, as I lay in my bed crying, I heard a noise outside my door. I waited in the darkness of my room to see who was there. The door cracked open just enough to see the hallway light, and I saw my father's figure there. In a soft, quiet voice he said, "I just wanted to let you know I love you. I love you just the way you are."

He shut the door and went to bed. I cried like I had never cried before. Until that moment, my daddy had never told me he loved me.

When he died many years later, I recalled that moment and the gift he had given me. It was the best and most important gift any father could give his daughter.

—SUSAN LINGO SPENCE

*Susan is a newlywed, married to a wonderful man who has two beautiful children who love Susan as much as she loves them. Susan works at a hospital and at age forty-six has returned to school to pursue her registered nursing license. She is happy, cancer-free, and feels very blessed.*

# Elijah

ONE RECENT MORNING OUR FEISTY, RAMBUNCTIOUS SIXTEEN-MONTH-OLD, Elijah, pulled a chair over to the water cooler on the kitchen counter and opened the spigot, laughing with glee as the water poured all over him and the floor. Such willful behavior was nothing new; it was present even before he was born.

Following the birth of our daughter Elana in 1996, my husband, Stephen, and I agreed we were done having children. I'd given birth to Elana's older sister, Sarah, sixteen months earlier, and we were also raising two teenage boys from Stephen's first marriage. Sarah was born at home, and we had planned the same for Elana, but complications put me into the hospital for the birth. We decided I would get my tubes tied while I was there.

Elana arrived in the world at 7 A.M.. The hospital staff scheduled me for the surgery at 4 P.M., telling me I couldn't eat anything the rest of the day because of the impending surgery. Hungry enough from labor to eat an entire large pizza by myself, I told my husband we were going home with our new baby. I'd come back some other time to get tied up. We weren't going to be making love anytime soon, anyway!

We rescheduled the procedure. However, a few days before the planned event, I came down with the worst case of flu in my life. I thought I was going to die. It took more than three weeks to recover from the flu, during which surgery was out of the question. We needed to again reschedule the procedure. Like the girl who cried wolf, I didn't know whether the doctor would believe me if I scheduled it a third time. Also, since I was experiencing my first and only bout with the flu in my life, I was beginning to wonder if God was giving me a message.

Soon after recovering from the flu, I returned to my daily practice of swimming laps at the health club. As I swam my laps, I suddenly experienced the presence of a little boy, telling me he wanted to come into our family. I even knew his name—Elijah. According to him, my husband and I were not finished having children. Elijah wanted to be born, and he wanted us as his family. I kept trying to push him away, but his energy was palpable to me, and he kept pulling me back.

When I got home, I told my husband about my experience. He gave me *the look* and basically said, "That's interesting, Dear. Get over it." Having another child was not up for discussion. Nineteen years already existed between his oldest and youngest children, and the idea of parenting three babies under age four seemed too much to consider. Feeling superstitious, we avoided having relations during the most fertile time of my cycle, and we increased our diligence with birth control. We decided one of us needed to be "fixed" very soon and so made plans.

From that day forward, the little boy, Elijah, was with me all the time, speaking to me at any moment I would listen. I felt trapped, but wanted to do the right thing. We were broke, tired, and maxed out. My husband definitely wasn't open to a conversation about having another child just because I was hearing voices.

The next month, my period was late. The only other time in my adult life I had been late was when I was carrying my girls. I knew I was pregnant with Elijah. While my husband was at work, I took a home pregnancy test to confirm what I already knew. The bright blue check mark popped out in less than a minute. Elijah had willed his way into our family despite our fears and objections. A wise soul, he knew better than we did that this was the right decision.

That evening, after putting Sarah and Elana to bed, I handed my husband a brandy and uttered the words every man dreads, "Honey, we need to talk." He already suspected; he knew I was late. I told him simply, "I am pregnant." I waited for the eruption. God bless him, he only took my hand and calmly said, "Okay." He knew, too, that this was something much larger than the two of us.

Three months into the pregnancy, while preparing for bed, a gush of water rushing down my leg alarmed me. I cried for my husband, called a neighbor to stay in the house with our sleeping babies, and raced with my husband to the emergency room. The doctor told us she was going to insert a piece of litmus paper into the area where the fluid was leaking. If the paper turned purple, the fluid was amniotic, which indicated the fetus was in trouble. We held our breaths, and before our eyes the paper turned quickly, and vividly, purple. I started to sob, and my husband looked grim. The medical staff gave Elijah a 10–20 percent chance of survival and sent me to bed, as we prayed for a miracle.

Although we hadn't asked for another child, God had placed him with us. We could have welcomed this turn of events—a natural way of eliminating the problem of an unwanted pregnancy. However, both my husband and I had fallen in love with the little soul developing within me. We'd fight for his life.

Upon returning from the hospital at 1 A.M., I sent an urgent e-mail message to thousands of subscribers to an online newsletter I publish, *The Entrepreneurial Couples Success Newsletter.* I asked for their prayers for Elijah. Over the next two days, we were flooded with hundreds of prayers by e-mail, fax, and phone from all over the world. Subscribers of all faiths not only prayed for Elijah directly, but they also passed the request on to their rabbis, ministers, priests, and prayer groups all kinds.

Three days later, my husband drove me to the follow-up doctor's appointment. We braced ourselves for bad news, but intuitively, I believed I was fine and Elijah had made it. Ah, the relief and joy in hearing the physician's words, "I see no evidence of any amniotic fluid loss. Your baby is completely fine. I wonder if you were misdiagnosed by the doctor you saw in emergency." My husband and I had witnessed the litmus paper turning purple. We knew this was no misdiagnosis—it was a miracle. Our prayers and the prayers of others for Elijah had been answered. He had again fought to be born and won.

My pregnancy continued uneventfully. On March 29, 1998, I gave birth at home, as planned, to Elijah Mordecai Jaffe, a healthy, beautiful little boy. We cannot imagine our family as being complete without him. Thank God this willful child insisted on being born into our family. He is far more of a blessing than he is the burden we had feared—even when he climbs on the kitchen table and throws food on the floor and then yanks the family computer keyboard off the desk just to hear it crash. Every time he exerts his will, which happens about one hundred times a day, we remind ourselves that the force of his soul and his personality are what brought him here to begin with.

Although we appreciate the blessings God has bestowed upon us, shortly after Elijah's birth my husband kept his appointment for the much-needed surgical procedure. I couldn't seem to get the job done.

—AZRIELA JAFFE

*Azriela lives in Lancaster, Pennsylvania, with Elijah, his two active, older sisters, Sarah and Elana, a teenage exchange student, and her husband, Stephen. Elijah continues to be a challenge on a daily basis.*

# Innocent Faith

THE CLACKING SOUND OF TRAIN WHEELS AROUSED ME FROM SLEEP. I LAY in the early morning, listening to the song of metal against metal, its cadence lulling, soothing, and tranquil, transporting me on a journey through time to my childhood in the 1940s.

The nation was warring without and festering within. Wartime industries nourished the U.S. economy, and unrest, fear, and indignation over the atrocities in Europe filled the country's citizenry. Meanwhile, here at home, to be black was to "step back."

With great remorse, my people now reflect back on those days of segregated train rides, substandard accommodations, and box lunches below the Mason–Dixon line. The connotations were intense and painful: We were second-class citizens, not good enough to ride in comfort or to eat in dignity with other Americans.

As a little girl off on a vacation, however, I traveled within the warmth of my family's love and care, protected from the sociological blight. A trip south brought me high anticipation.

Mother had packed our lunch, carefully wrapping pieces of fried chicken and bread in neat squares of waxed paper and placing them in a brown paper bag. She had combined celery stalks and carrot sticks with fruit in another bag; chunks of wrapped chocolate cake went into a third. Mother embedded all three bags in a cushion of napkins placed in a suitcase. She then tied the case with a cord, because it had a broken lock that someone could easily open in a moment of hunger.

I loved the train's rollicking sway from side to side. I walked up and down the aisle, trying to balance myself and occasionally falling into someone's lap when the train lurched. I chatted with neighboring riders about my vacation expectations: cousins to see; berries to pick; cows to milk; pigs to chase; and bunnies, kittens, and chicks to fondle. Every summer, I experienced all the excitement of a city girl's once-a-year visit to the country. Mother finally enticed me to sit down and enjoy my storybooks, which I never traveled without.

The conductor took the tickets and asked my age.

"I'm seven," I piped up. "And I'm going to have my birthday at my grandma's house in Denmark." The conductor nodded indulgently, his droll expression indicating his relief in not having to put up with my chatter throughout the trip.

"You'll have to change in Raleigh," he said to Mother. "This train's not going any farther than there."

Mother became upset. "But, we booked a through train," she said, her voice quavering nervously. "We were told we wouldn't have to change in Washington as we usually do and could go straight through to South Carolina."

"Well, part of the train's going through, but this here part is being turned around in Raleigh and heading back the other way. You'll have to change there and get the next one out from Washington. You'll be laid over for about two hours." The conductor stated the edict, snipped the ticket, and walked away.

He didn't look back to see the muscles twitching in Mother's face or the eyes welling up with tears as she fought for control. She heaved a sigh and looked away from me. My eyes never missed a thing, and my ears sensitively interpreted the emotional tone of the conversation.

Mother disliked the idea of sitting for two hours on the "colored" side of the southern station platform. She felt even stronger against going into the segregated waiting room, which seemed never to have seen a broom or a mop. With no ventilation or disinfectant, the room held all the fetid odors of the tired, weary patrons who had trekked in and out of it for weeks, months, or maybe years. Mother knew the restrooms would be untidy and unclean, assaulting her meticulous senses and degrading the dignified lessons of hygiene she had taught her child. Two hours might well be two days. The notion made her distraught.

I watched my mother closely for a while, then turned my face to the window and looked out at the passing scenery. Since I had become quiet and withdrawn, Mother thought I had dozed off.

The train continued its journey, past Petersburgh and Richmond, across the North Carolina border, and ever closer to Raleigh. Mother, organized as ever, began to gather up our belongings, so she could embark with a minimal amount of difficulty. I sat complacent and comfortable, not moving to help.

"You'd better get your things together," Mother said. "We'll be coming into Raleigh soon," and you won't want to have to scramble for things."

Still, I continued to sit as the train began to lose speed on its approach to the station.

"Come on, Dear," Mother urged, her voice becoming somewhat stern.

"No, Mother," I said to her. "We don't have to change. I know. I talked to God, and I told Him I knew you were worried about changing, so I know we won't."

Mother's eyes again filled with tears. She didn't know how to respond to my little-girl resolve and how to meet this test of faith. Her own faith had been tried and weakened. What could she say?

The conductor came down the aisle. "Raleigh! Raleigh! Next stop, Raleigh!" he called. He approached Mother, who stood reaching toward the rack for her bags.

"You and your little girl can stay on," he said to Mother. "Plans have changed, and they decided to send this whole train through. Just take your seats and get comfortable."

Mother looked at me. My face had broken into a great big grin; my impish body bounced up and down. "I knew it," I cried. "I told you so. I knew it, because God told me."

—REBECCA HAYES

*From this early experience Rebecca learned to lean on prayer and faith as her guide through life. Now sixty-six years old, with four children and four grandchildren, her undying faith is her legacy to her family.*

# The Playhouse

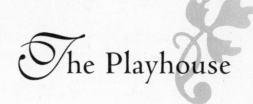

MY BROTHER, FRANK, AND I GREW UP IN CHERRY HILL, A SUBDIVISION on the outskirts of Baltimore, Maryland. We were one of the first families to move to Cherry Hill.

One beautiful spring morning, when I was nine and Frank was eight, Frank left the house very early. I usually went everywhere he did, but I had chores to do and he didn't, because he was a boy.

When Frank came back in the house later that morning, he told me he wanted to show me something. I did everything with Frank, because he had such a wonderful imagination. So I readily went with him, eager to see what new thing he'd found.

We crossed the railroad tracks across from our house and went into the woods, with Frank leading the way. He was impatient for me to hurry, but I was getting a little nervous, because we were going deeper into the woods than we ever had before.

Finally, we came to a little clearing surrounded by tall trees laden with pink apple blossoms. Their sweet perfume filled the air. In the center of clearing stood some sort of shelter made of big cardboard boxes. Frank grabbed my hand and pulled me into the "playhouse," as he called it.

I don't know how long he had been bringing the boxes into the woods, cutting out windows, and making the floor, which an old blanket partially covered. I asked him how he had done all of it without my knowledge. He just grinned his beautiful smile and looked all-knowing as we sat on the old blanket and looked out the makeshift windows of our playhouse. After Frank was satisfied he had duly impressed me with his efforts, we went and sat outside the playhouse.

I still remember the feeling and smell of the cool grass as we lay with our hands behind our heads, looking up at what I thought was heaven. Beautiful sun rays streamed through the towering trees, so high we couldn't see their tops, and the smell of the apple blossoms enveloped us.

We knew no one had been to this spot before us. It was our special magic place.

Frank and I talked into the afternoon—sitting on the grass, going in and out of our playhouse, naming the things we'd bring back to decorate it more. On that first day in our playhouse, we dreamed of a long and glorious life for us both. There in our hideaway that summer of 1959, with a new era just around the corner, our dreams had just begun.

—Patricia Howard Fong

*Tragically, Pat lost her brother eight years later when he unexpectedly died at the young age of sixteen. She is grateful now for this memory, and for the love, laughter, and innocence she experienced that day in their playhouse. Now forty-nine, Patricia is a wife, mother of two, and grandmother of four. She is an Equal Employment Opportunity specialist with the federal government. Pat writes poetry and enjoys family genealogy.*

# Forever in Her Debt

THE SILENCE OF THE CALM NIGHT WAS BROKEN BY FIRE ENGINES ROARING by. I don't remember what I was doing at the time, but I vividly remember what happened later.

When I went to the home that was burning down, I saw a member of the congregation where I preached standing on the opposite side of the street. I went over to stand beside her. Frantic, she insisted her son was still in the house, even though people had assured her he had escaped. Unfortunately, she was right. Her son never made it out.

I had just starting my preaching job there and was quite young. The day after the fire, I went to see the grieving mother in preparation for the funeral service. What do you say? Admittedly dumbfounded at the moment, I couldn't seem to find the words of consolation.

Then she spoke.

She said her husband had preceded her in death several years earlier and later her other son had died in the war. She'd lost her only remaining family member, her son, in that awful fire. Still unable to speak, I placed my hand gently on her shoulder, and she said something that will stay with me for as long as I live.

In the face of such tragedy, she said, "The Lord giveth, and the Lord taketh away; blessed be the name of the Lord." Oh, I knew those words. I had used them myself in talking, writing, and preaching, but they had a special meaning that day.

I honestly don't know how I would respond if I was dealt a loss such as hers, but I hope I could express those faith-affirming words and go on. She could have given up. She could have blamed God or the fire department. She could have resigned herself to slowly die in anguish. She chose none of those options.

Thirty years later, I remember that moment as one of the most valuable lessons I have ever learned. I shall forever be in her debt for faith's greatest "sermon."

—LARRY HARP

*Larry lives in Texas with his lovely wife, a native of Fort Worth. Larry writes song lyrics and poetry and is currently working on a book titled* This One Thing I Do. *Larry serves as a substitute preacher in several congregations and is an accomplished song director. Although Larry has suffered many physical difficulties for some years now, his faith is bolstered and his strength is maintained by a wonderful Christian woman who once said, "The Lord giveth, and the Lord taketh away; blessed be the name of the Lord."*

# Cat Angel

ON OCTOBER 2, 1999, MY SEVENTEEN-YEAR-OLD SON, TONY, CELEBRATED his second anniversary of being seizure free following brain surgery. This story is not about Tony; it's about his guardian angel.

When Tony was just a baby, a guardian angel walked into our lives. The angel, like Tony, was just a year old—and a cat. The kitty bonded with my son immediately.

For sixteen years our cat watched over Tony. Whenever he sensed Tony was about to seizure, which happened often in those days, he would tear through the house, calling me and leading me to wherever Tony was.

Then he would sit on top of Tony, preventing him from getting up and endangering himself, and wait for the seizure to come. After the seizure stopped, he would nuzzle near Tony's ear, purring him back to reality.

We all faced many challenges over the years, until finally, two years ago, my son underwent brain surgery that changed his life forever.

Since then, Tony has had no seizures. In fact, as of this writing, the doctors have finally allowed us to use the word "cured."

Last night, as if knowing his work here was done, our dear guardian angel slept his final sleep. We held him as he died, telling him we loved him, would miss him, and that one day we'd all be together in heaven.

When I awoke this morning, I realized we had actually experienced two miracles in our lives. Tony had been cured of epilepsy, and a little guardian angel had watched over him all those years.

He was a true friend. We will miss him.

—JUDY GUARINO

*Judy and Tony Guarino are dealing with the loss of their guardian angel. They know they will meet him at the "rainbow bridge" when they arrive in heaven.*

# 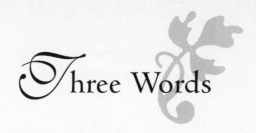Three Words

WHEN I WAS THREE YEARS OLD, MY PARENTS DISCOVERED I WAS TOTALLY deaf, a situation that forced them to make crucial decisions about my education. They decided to "mainstream" me, which meant that all of my peers and teachers would have normal hearing.

I was the only deaf child at Blue Creek Elementary School in the small, quiet town of Latham, New York. From almost my first day there, the other kids taunted me and called me names because of my hearing aid and the way I talked. I remember thinking, "What have I done wrong?"

My hearing aid consisted of a rectangular box that was harnessed to my shoulders and hung from my neck like an albatross. It created a big lump on my chest, with wires running from the box to my ears.

I experienced great anxiety throughout elementary school, because, not only did I struggle to fit in with the other students, I also grappled mightily with most of my schoolwork. I seemed to spend every spare moment doing homework just so I could keep up. The teachers didn't know what to do with me.

Mrs. Jordan, my fifth grade teacher, changed all that with a simple three-word phrase.

A large woman with salt-and-pepper hair and twinkling brown eyes, Mrs. Jordan had a voice that boomeranged off the walls of her tiny classroom. One morning she asked the class a question. I read her lips from my front-row seat and immediately raised my hand.

For once I knew the answer. I will never forget what happened next. Her response was explosive. It startled all of us. Mrs. Jordan enthusiastically slammed her right foot on the floor and whirled her right finger in a full circle until it pointed directly at me. With sparkling eyes and a wide smile she exclaimed, "That's right, Stephen!"

For the first time in my young life, I felt like an instant star. My heart burst with pride as an ear-to-ear grin filled my face. I sat a little taller in my chair and puffed out my chest. My confidence soared like never before.

From that day forward, my grades and speech improved dramatically. My popularity among my peers increased, and my outlook on life did a complete turnabout.

I never forgot Mrs. Jordan.

Thirty years later, as I sat in my living room, feeling particularly grateful for all my success as a former Wall Street stockbroker turned inspirational speaker and author, I decided to express my gratitude to Mrs. Jordan in a big way, perhaps on national television. I sent a letter to eight different national talk shows and within a week, I heard back from three of them. The *Leeza* show, based in Hollywood, quickly arranged to fly us out on separate planes for a surprise reunion.

Initially, it was difficult to get Mrs. Jordan to come to the show, because she is one of those dedicated teachers who never missed a day in the classroom. Her husband, daughter, and even the principal got involved and, without revealing the true nature of the trip, convinced her to go on the show. She finally relented and flew out with her daughter.

On the day of taping, Leeza asked me what Mrs. Jordan had done to turn my life around, and I told her my story. Then I was instructed to hide backstage while they brought out Mrs. Jordan. The camera followed her apprehensive face to her seat. Leeza asked if she knew why she was there. The teacher replied she did not. Leeza told Mrs. Jordan that someone had written a letter telling them she had made a very big difference in this person's life.

Leeza then played a tape of a recording I had done earlier in the green room. While the tape played, a flicker of recognition crossed Mrs. Jordan's face. Leeza turned to Mrs. Jordan and asked if she recognized the voice. To everyone's astonishment—including my own—she said, "Yes, that was Stephen Hopson." I couldn't believe she would remember my name after all these years! At that moment, I leapt on stage to greet her.

Incredibly, Mrs. Jordan is still teaching in the same classroom where I was once a pupil. As she and her daughter were flying home afterward, the pilot, who had heard about her being on the show, made an announcement to the other passengers. They erupted into loud cheers and applause for her. On the day the show aired, the entire elementary school filed into the auditorium to watch the show with her.

I've gone on to pursue a lifelong dream of becoming an inspirational speaker and author. I have no doubt that the gift I give my audiences started with the gift Mrs. Jordan gave me over thirty years ago.

—STEPHEN J. HOPSON

*Stephen is currently working on his first book,* Goodbye, Wall Street! *When not traveling and speaking, he is a lay minister at the Church of Today in Michigan, where bestselling author Marianne Williamson is the lead minister.*

# Don't Let Life Pass You By

ALL OF US KIDS KNEW GRANDMA NEEDED SPECIAL HELP TO GET AROUND. When we saw her coming outside, we rushed across the yard and offered our arm to help support her, so she wouldn't lose her balance and fall. I remember as a six-year-old child slowing my pace to match hers and trying to walk beside her to wherever she wanted to go.

My grandma had been injured as a child while skating, and one of her legs was longer than the other one. For as long as I'd known her, she had walked with a limp, using first a cane and then a walker. As she grew older, the pain from walking in such an unnatural way became constant, and she eventually became wheelchair bound.

Grandma hated being a burden to anybody. Once she required the wheelchair, she rarely left the house. She spent the next thirty years of her life sitting next to a window in her living room, going outside only to see a doctor or to attend an important family occasion. Grandma feared many things, including the surgeries that could have helped her lead a more normal life. Because she knew the physical therapy she badly needed would hurt intensely, she put it off until her body was too old to handle the surgeries.

The saddest part about Grandma wasn't the physical pain she endured, it was her isolation and self-absorption. When she spoke to people, the only thing she could relate to was the pain she was going through, so she shared it with anybody who would listen. As a child, I couldn't figure out why she did this, because it didn't change how much pain she was in and no one seemed to care anyway. Growing up, I watched Grandma alienate everyone around her and promised myself I would keep whatever pain I might experience private.

Perhaps I have painted a rather negative picture of my grandma, but I loved her the way a child always adores his or her grandma. I loved her for never forgetting my birthday and for sending me one of her special cards with a dollar for each year of my life enclosed. I still remember the feel of the warm pajamas she gave us as children every Christmas, when Mom and Dad could not afford to get us any. No matter how much pain she was in, Grandma never missed a graduation, wedding, or any other special event in our lives.

The greatest gift my grandma gave me came later, when I was no longer a little girl and had become a woman.

She came to visit me in the hospital after I'd undergone surgery for a herniated disc that had troubled me for eight years. When my grandma spoke to me of her pain that time, it was different.

She quietly told me, "Terri, I have been hurting all my life. I let my pain get me down and missed so much. The one thing I have always admired about you is that no matter how badly you hurt, you always get up and do something with your life. Don't ever sit down and let life pass you by the way I did."

My Grandma Zenna passed away soon after that conversation. I pulled myself out of that hospital bed and worked hard on my recovery. I didn't complain about the pain much to others.

Sometimes a role model comes along who teaches more by the example of what she is not than by what she is. My grandma showed me that focusing entirely on your suffering can ruin your life. I refuse to let pain be my master.

Grandma remains a positive role model for me in many other ways too. Despite her suffering, she also taught me about honesty, commitment, compassion, and loyalty.

I never really knew until that moment by my bedside that my grandma had regrets. Though she is gone now, she still helps me to live my life with no regrets. Grandma Zenna taught me, above all else, that life is short, precious, and not to be wasted.

—TERESA ANNKLEIN BEAVER

*Terri was a single mother at the time of her surgery and during most of the eight years she had a herniated disc. She attributes her strength to the love and dedication she has for her children, Robbie, Carrie, and Logan. She recently moved and married a wonderful man named Joe. Her husband has two great sons, Ash and Ant, who have taught Terri that love reaches out with open arms to include everyone and to make a truly happy family.*

# Asleep at the Wheel

I PACED THE FLOOR—SOMETHING I RARELY HAD TO DO WHEN IT CAME TO my daughter, Kellie. When she was running late, she always called to let me know where she was. She should have been home hours ago!

A sinking feeling that something awful had happened gripped me. She was driving home from camp, where she was a counselor for kids with cancer. It was a two-and-a-half-hour drive, and I had expected her home by 6:30 that evening.

Nine o'clock came and went, and still I hadn't heard from her. I imagined every ill fate known to humankind. So, I walked the floor, praying I'd see her car coming down the road or pulling into the drive.

Shortly after 11:00 P.M., I called the highway patrol and nearby hospitals. They had no reports on Kellie, but the police promised to keep an eye out for her car. I was beside myself with fear and guilt. "If only I'd just driven her myself," I admonished myself. I sat on the couch and tried to watch television, but I couldn't concentrate on anything but Kellie.

Somehow, I fell asleep.

Suddenly, I awoke startled! Confused at first, then quickly remembering my fears, I jumped up from the couch and ran into the kitchen. How could I have fallen asleep when my oldest child was missing? An overpowering feeling of fear consumed me; I knew something was terribly wrong. I looked at the kitchen clock: it was 1:10 A.M.! I fell to my knees and began praying, "Please God, don't let anything happen to her. Send an angel to sit closely beside her and bring her safely home."

I resumed my pacing, again looking out at the quiet, dark night. At 2:40 A.M., I spotted the glow of headlights. When Kellie's car pulled into the driveway, I began weeping and ran outside. She was home and alive, and that's all I cared about for the moment.

Kellie recounted how she had taken the wrong exit and driven for hours in the wrong direction. She had retraced her path to find the proper exit, but grew too tired to stay awake.

Her eyes filled with tears as she continued her story. "Mom, I was so tired, I kept dozing off. Then, for some reason, I glanced over at the passenger seat, and I saw a man who looked just like Granddad sitting in my car!"

My father had passed away only five months before.

"The next thing I knew, I was sitting in my parked car on the shoulder of the opposite side of the road. I don't know how I got there.

Deep ditches lined both sides of the road, and the car had come to a stop less than two feet from a utility pole. It was quiet and dark. The only thing I noticed was the green glow from the dashboard clock. Granddad was gone, and I was alone in the car."

I hugged my precious daughter and through my tears asked, "What time did the clock read?"

"Mom," Kellie replied, "I'll never forget the time. It was 1:16 A.M."

"1:16!—just six minutes from the time I prayed for God to send an angel to your side!"

There was no question in our minds that Kellie's angel—my father—had saved her life. My prayers had been answered.

—ROBIN NISIUS

*Robin Nisius lives with her husband and children in Northeast Iowa, where she and her husband own and operate a recording studio. Robin works part-time as a nurse at the student health center of a local university. She writes short stories and songs.*

# Beautiful Eyebrows

MY MOTHER-IN-LAW LAY COMATOSE IN THE INTENSIVE CARE UNIT, HOOKED up to every piece of life support equipment the hospital offered. A bout of the flu had complicated her emphysema, which until then had been undiagnosed. Now it looked like she might die. Hour by hour, another of her vital organs shut down. The only one still working was her strong heart.

According to the doctor, we could do nothing but watch and wait. Normally a talkative bunch, we now had nothing to say. "Because she's so tiny, I can only give her medication a drop at a time," the doctor said. "It's like pushing a wet noodle along a table."

None of us wanted to admit what was on our minds, but it was obvious from our faces that we each feared the worst. The mood in the room was grim; it was hard to smile even when one of the members of our local clergy stopped by to offer support and prayers.

After some time, my mother-in-law's nurse came in. She moved with authority, checking on each piece of machinery. At one point, I counted more than a dozen different lines and machines. When she was through, I expected her to simply leave quietly. Instead, she went to the head of the bed and stood there for a moment, studying my mother-in-law's face. Then very, very gently, she reached down and brushed a stray hair from her face. It was an act so unexpectedly tender and kind, it startled me. "She has beautiful eyebrows," she said gently. Then she turned and left the room.

I stood there, dumbfounded. Beautiful eyebrows. All I could see were machines. Then, for the first time since my mother-in-law had gotten sick, I saw the woman rather than her illness.

—ROBIN SILVERMAN

*With good medicine and several prayer chains, Robin's mother-in-law recovered and went on to enjoy five more years of life. She passed away from emphysema in October 1999. Even when she was totally bedridden, her eyebrows still danced whenever someone she loved entered the room.*

# The Bathtub

I WANTED TO TAKE A NICE HOT BATH AND READ A BOOK A FRIEND HAD loaned me, called *Reaching the Summit,* by Pat Summitt. Tired and a little stressed, all I wanted to do was lie in the hottest water I could stand and lose myself in the book—but "Aqua Boy" had other ideas. Aqua Boy lives in our house in the form of my son, Caleb. When he realized what I was going to do, he started asking to take a bath too. Of course, I said no.

"Oh, Pleazzzzzzzzzzzze, Daddy?"

"Caleb, I said no."

"But I wannnnnaaa!"

After a few hundred no's I told him I would think about it.

I climbed into the bathtub and turned on the water. AHHHHH-HHHH!! This was going to be relaxing. Suddenly, there was Aqua Boy. He had asked his mom, my wife, Kristi, if he could take a bath with me after I was done. She told him to go ask Daddy. So there he was, with big old puppy dog eyes that still had tears in them.

"Daddy, can I take a bath with you when you're done?" I knew I was trapped.

"Okay," I said. "When Daddy is done, you can come in here with me."

His eyes lit up, and he said, "That'll be great!"

I went back to my book. The next time I looked up he had taken off all his clothes and had plopped himself up on the toilet with his feet on the seat squatting down like a catcher. I looked at my naked son and asked him, "What are you doing?"

"I'm waiting for you to be done."

"Caleb, when I'm done, I'll call for you. Then you can come in. Okay?"

"Okay, Daddy."

He left, and I went back to my book—until he returned to the bathroom again. This time, he carried the toy fishing pole he had gotten for Christmas.

"What are you doing, Caleb?"

"I'm just watching you."

"Caleb, you need to leave until I call you."

He pulled up his little stool that we keep in the bathroom to help him reach the sink when he's brushing his teeth. He plopped his naked buttocks down on it.

"Caleb, you can't come into the tub until I am done."

"I know, Daddy. I'll just sit here and wait until you are done."

There he sat, like Opie from *The Andy Griffith Show,* with his fishing pole and his really bad haircut from the week before that makes his ears stick out.

I got back to my book. In the meantime, my wife sat out in the kitchen, listening to all of this and grinning. By then, it was really hard to concentrate on my book. I had only twenty minutes before I had to get ready for work, and I was really looking forward to relaxing. I tried to concentrate on the words.

PLOP! I looked down in the water to see a great big, plastic Fisher Price hook, connected to a colorful Fisher Price Fishing Pole, connected to the little hands of my bare son.

"Caleb, you can't go fishing in the bathtub right now. Daddy is trying to take his bath."

"I'm sorry; I'm sorry; I'm sorry." (Caleb always apologizes in threes.)

Instead of leaving, he just sat there on his stool. I tried to read, but it was getting harder and harder.

"Caleb, what are you doing now?"

"I'm just gonna' sit here and wait for you to get done."

I tried to read one last time, but couldn't. He just sat there next to the bathtub, staring at me with those big brown "doe" eyes, his new fishing pole over his shoulder.

Minute by minute, he had slowly and methodically broken me down and reduced me to emotional mush. My son is not a very patient three-year-old. I guess not many are. But I couldn't believe how patient he was being. My heart went out to him.

"Caleb, do you want to come in the bathtub now?"

"That would be great!"

"Okay, come on in."

Then we had a great twenty minutes of splashing, fishing, and being kids together.

—MICHAEL T. POWERS

*Michael is happily married to Kristi, his high school sweetheart. They have two sons, Caleb and Connor. He owns a video production business, coaches high school girl's basketball, and loves to write in his "spare" time.*

# $\mathcal{L}$addie McCrea

IN 1987, I WAS A YOUNG COMPUTER PROFESSIONAL WITH A PASSION FOR photographing interesting faces and places. I took a month leave from work and purchased a thirty-day Greyhound bus pass. My trip began in Orlando, Florida, with a Cannon A1, thirty rolls of film, a change of clothes, and fifty dollars. I really had no idea where I was going, where I would stay, or how the fifty dollars would last thirty days. My only plan was to venture Northwest and to experience America—everything else would take care of itself.

The trip created many life-long memories of interesting people and exciting places. Some of the most earnest memories were born in Seattle, where I met Laddie.

Laddie was a hobo.

He was between sixty and seventy years old, but looked a hundred. His scraggly, shoulder-length, white hair was entangled with weeds from the previous night's bedding. His clothes were a living journal of evenings in the shrubs and days in the sun, and he smelled of alcohol and urine.

When I first met Laddie, he was standing on a busy downtown Seattle sidewalk, greeting every passerby with a smile, a pleasant comment, and an extended palm. Each day, society rushed past Laddie, either unaware of his existence or avoiding what they saw in him—a smelly, begging bum.

I decided Laddie was an excellent character for my photo excursion, so I paid him to allow me to stand in the background and film him. I spent three days hidden in the masses, photographing Laddie. Most of the time, he was unaware of my existence.

One special day, as I observed from a bench off in the distance, a young girl of around six or seven, prim and proper with a pretty dress and her hair in a ponytail, approached Laddie from behind and tugged on his shirt. Laddie turned to the girl, who then reached up and handed him something.

At that, Laddie, in animated fashion, showed his happiness and reached in his pocket and gave her something. The girl ran back to her parents, excitedly showing them what she had received.

I was curious about the exchange and dying to go immediately over to ask Laddie what took place, but to get candid photos, I couldn't make my presence known. Later that afternoon when I finished my shoot, I asked him about the little girl.

He told me, "The little girl came to me and gave me a quarter, so I gave her two quarters in return. I wanted to show her that when you are generous, you will receive more than you give."

Laddie had a wonderful look, and I was blessed with the opportunity to capture him on film, but he gave me much more than interesting pictures to adorn my walls. He taught me a lesson in humanity. He showed me we all have something to offer and it's not a matter of social status; it's a matter of finding our gift and taking the time to share it.

—MIKE KLEIMAN

*Thirteen years later, Mike is still a computer professional but his greater passion now is raising his two young children. He believes that if he can somehow teach his children what Laddie taught him, he'll be a success.*

# Wubber Wooban

SHE WAS ALMOST THREE YEARS OLD, WITH LONG RINGLETS OF HAIR THE exact color of honey and a cute little dimple in her cheek. Her name was Angela, but my mom had only named her that so she could call her "Angel." She was my baby sister.

I was ten and having a rough summer. My parents were divorcing; my older sister, Lisa, and I weren't getting along, and Angel had been sick for a month. Even though she had only a cold, her usual robust, cheerful zest for life was gone. She seemed to have just lost interest in everything around her. She no longer jumped off the couch, yelling a startling "Wubber Wooban!" (her hero, Wonder Woman). She seemed so quiet and sleepy all the time.

One hot June day, Mom announced she felt very strongly that Angel did not have just a cold, and she set off, pushing Angel in the stroller, to see our family doctor. I watched them walk away until I could see them no more, while in my eyes the sun made mirage lakes in the hot, black pavement.

They didn't come home until late that night. Alone and frightened for our baby sister, Lisa and I waited anxiously for hours. Dad had also gone to the doctor's, and when I saw his car pull into the driveway, I knew something was wrong. Both my parents were crying. I had never seen my dad cry. Their words "cancer" and "leukemia" swirled around in my head. Mom was on the phone. Friends were coming over. Everyone was crying.

Angel stayed in the hospital a long time. We weren't allowed to see her for a while. When we finally did, Mom or Dad carried her out to us in the waiting room of the University of California–Davis Medical Center. We weren't allowed into the wing, because if we spread germs to any of the sick kids, they could die. Mom held Angel out for us to gently kiss and hug for only a moment. She was so frail. It was then my ten-year-old mind grasped that my baby sister could die.

She almost did. It was terrifying. She needed radiation and chemotherapy, which meant a forty-five-minute drive every day to Sacramento. Too poor since my dad had left to own a car, my mom had no way to get to the hospital, and my father was unable to take Angel for her treatments. Without them, she could die.

We prayed for a way to get Angel to the hospital—a tall order, since she had to go every single day! It was then I learned that the Lord takes care of us by sending people to do His work.

The people from our church appeared like angels. Not only did they organize daily rides for Angel's treatments, but they also always stopped at McDonald's for Angel's favorite "hangubers"—every day! They also brought us meals and took us into their homes, and the entire congregation fasted and prayed together for her remission.

Angel's "cold" nearly took her life—and did take all of her beautiful, curly, honey-colored hair—but she did go into remission. It was a long road, but she made it.

My sister is now twenty-seven years old and married. In beating leukemia, she has blessed the lives of everyone around her. She is generous, thoughtful, and creative, and has a great laugh.

I thank God for the angels that provided the way for my little sister to live. They gave us a wonderful gift that truly lasts a lifetime.

—SUSAN FAHNCKE

*Susan and Angela are very close and both now live in northern Utah. Susan is a freelance writer. Angela works in retail and enjoys many hobbies and activities with her husband. She has been in remission for over twenty-three years.*

# Mother's Silver Candlesticks

MY MOTHER SAW THE CANDLESTICKS DISPLAYED ON A SHELF IN THE REAR of a secondhand store in the tenement district of New York City. They were approximately ten inches tall and heavily tarnished, but a surreptitious rub revealed their possibility, and a glance at the base showed the magic word "sterling." How did they get there? What poor soul had hocked them to survive? Mother ached to buy them, but we had come to exchange the shoes I was wearing for another pair to fit my growing feet. First things came first.

New York, where we settled upon entering the United States, and the area where we lived bore little resemblance to the *Goldene Medina,* the golden land, that many immigrants had envisioned in their dreams. However, it was a land of opportunities, where all might achieve their aspirations if they worked hard toward their goals.

"We can swim, or we can sink," declared Mutti, as I called my mother, "and I have always been a strong swimmer."

And swim we did! Dad peddled caramelized almonds, which we made each evening and packed into cellophane bags, up and down Broadway. Mother went to school in the morning to learn to be a masseuse and did housework for various families several afternoons a week. I attended school at PS–51. My sister, Lotte, went to the Institute for the Deaf in St. Louis, where she worked in an exchange program to learn English. Some nights Dad worked as a night watchman, Mother sewed leather gloves for a manufacturing firm, and I strung beaded necklaces for the Woolworth store for one cent apiece.

The fifth-floor walk-up apartment we shared on 150th and Riverside Drive was hardly what my parents had been used to in their native country, Germany. It really wasn't a walk up—it had an elevator—but the man who ran it held out his hand for tips each time anyone wanted a ride. Who could afford donations? We walked upstairs.

The place consisted of a kitchen, bathroom, living room, and one bedroom. My sister and I shared the double bed in the living room, until she went off to school. When we first viewed the apartment, my mom blanched at the filth of the place. But with determination and elbow grease we made it habitable.

The first evening we slept there, I woke up in the middle of the night, itching all over. My sister called my mother, thinking I was breaking out with measles, chicken pox, or some other ailment. I wasn't running a fever; I just had red spots all over. Dad took one look at me, said something I cannot repeat, took a knife, and made a slit in the mattress. It was alive. He pulled the sheets off the mattress. He dragged the mattress off our bed and through my parents' bedroom, and then tossed it out of the fifth-floor window to the street below, where it exploded.

I've often wondered where the bugs found shelter in New York's winter weather.

Lotte and I bedded down on the floor until morning, when Dad found a second-hand store where he exchanged his winter coat for another mattress. I remember Mom cried a lot.

During one of our nightly chats while working together, Mutti told me about the candlesticks.

"Let's see if we can manage to buy them. I think they could look good once we clean and polish them."

Together we schemed how to save enough money to purchase them for Daddy's birthday. Thinking back, it was not the gift my father would have chosen to receive. He was more interested in the war, what of his property he could salvage, and how we would eat and pay the rent. But Mom was desperate to have something of beauty in our dingy flat.

The candlesticks cost three dollars. We conceived our plan in March and discussed money-saving strategies.

"I'll see if I can talk our three elderly neighbors into letting me carry their trash down to the basement," I offered. Plus, I could make money stringing necklaces.

"I'll buy large eggs for Daddy, and we'll eat the smaller and cheaper ones," said Mom.

In addition, she purchased three-day-old bread, instead of day-old, saving seven cents a loaf. A friend told her that wrapping a damp cloth around the bread and heating it in the oven would make it taste fresh again. It worked!

We turned saving pennies into a game. At the end of April, we made a fifty-cent down payment on our treasure. By September 23, 1940, we proudly "paid them off," and the proprietor even threw in some used candles. The candlestick purchase provided our education in the American theory of "lay-away" and "charge account," which were so strange to people of my parents' background.

We rubbed and polished the silver. Mother cut the used candles and scraped the outside until they looked almost like new ones. I will never forget the first Sabbath Eve when we lit the tapers. Tears ran down my mother's face as she recited the blessings. Despite the hardships, we were grateful to be together and, most of all, to be safe and sound.

When I married and moved to Wyoming, my mother gave me the candlesticks as a wedding gift, so that I might always share in their beauty. "You helped to buy them. You know how much they mean to me. I want you to have them and to someday pass them on to your daughter," she said.

The candlesticks now stand on top of the piano in my living room. We have used them at every memorable occasion of our family's life, both happy and sad. One day, I will pass them on to my daughter, as they were passed along to me. The Sabbath candlesticks are, and always will be, much more than candlesticks. They are symbols of faith, courage, and love.

—LIESEL SHINEBERG

*Liesel's mother had a wonderful collection of antique silver in her home in Germany. The Shinebergs left behind their silver and other possessions when German authorities gave them eight hours to either leave the country or forfeit their exit visas. They took only what they could carry as they walked to the border. Because her mother mourned irreplaceable pictures and mementos, the candlesticks represented a wistful memory of long ago. Today they have a place of honor on Liesel's piano. Her younger daughter put her name on the bottom of one, and her girls know that someday they will light Nanny's candles as well.*

# Yard Sale

THIS PAST SATURDAY I HELPED MY UNCLE AND AUNT WITH THEIR YARD sale. My uncle enjoys going to estate auctions, and if a box of books goes cheaply enough, he buys them. He gives most of them away. He asked me to go through the books and pull out the inspirational and religious books to put into a box that said "Free."

Something drew me to open one particular small book. I was stunned to discover the forty-year-old book had belonged to the daughter of a lady in my church. An only child, she had died in a car accident more than thirty years ago! I recognized her name only because a few weeks earlier the woman had testified at our church's ladies night how God had helped her recover from losing her only child. At the time of her tragic death, the woman's daughter had been only twenty-five years old and six weeks away from her wedding date.

As soon as the yard sale was over, I ran over to their home to give them their daughter's book. The father was the only one home. I gave the book to him, and when he saw her name his eyes filled with tears. Concerned that I had upset him, I started to apologize.

He insisted, "No, it's all right. It's just that I was sitting here thinking about my little girl and how hard it was going to be to go through another Father's Day without her."

"Well," I said, "it looks like she was thinking of you too, because she sent you this Father's Day present!"

—CHERYL NORWOOD

*Cheryl is a desktop publisher for a large suburban Atlanta church. She wed her best friend, Mike, after fourteen years of knowing everything about one another. They have been married for ten years and are the proud slaves of one very silly Siamese cat named Princess Jasmine Poopalot. They live in a tiny World War II bungalow they call Luvbird Cottage and enjoy laughing, loving, and performing random acts of kindness.*

# Just Wanted to Talk

DEAR MOM,

It's now two months since your passing. I survived your funeral, made it through my first motherless Mother's Day, and am slowly re-entering everyday life. But I need to tell you, Mom, it's not easy.

I never thought of us as terribly close. We actually spent more time butting our Irish heads together than not. Affection was not part of our history either. The turn of your cheek as I kissed you comprised the sum of our physical interaction. But the one thing we could always do was talk—usually from opposite ends of the spectrum, mind you—nonetheless, we talked.

I called you every day. Our routines rarely varied. I'd ask about your lunch. You'd review CNN news. We'd talk about your grandchildren. Occasionally, you'd mention neighborhood happenings. Then I'd wish you good-night and say good-bye. For the last fifteen years, that was our routine.

Occasionally, the pattern changed. I would guiltily miss a day. You would take the initiative and call me. If I wasn't home, you refused to leave a message. You'd just hang up, muttering "damn machine." Eventually, you accepted modern technology and spoke. Your standard message was, "You know who I am. You know my number. Bye!" It was always a toss-up which I found more frustrating—your hang-ups or your messages.

In the fall of 1995, you fell ill. Time and a careless lifestyle sought their revenge. You required hospitalization. Doctors predicted the worst. "Not my mom," I thought. Little did they know about the strong-willed Irish woman lying in their sterile bed.

You survived and in time returned home. The daily patterns of our phone calls continued. You were indestructible. Or so it seemed to me.

Three years later, almost to the day, you again lost a skirmish against the vices battling for your body. Again you traveled to the hospital, and the doctors again predicted gloom and doom. "Not my mom," I insisted. "You don't know who you're dealing with."

This time, however, I was wrong. The advancing diseases consuming your body and mind would no longer allow you an independent lifestyle. Health officials warned me against bringing you into my home. They felt you were too difficult a patient to handle. Again I answered, "Not my mom."

I decided living together would make up for time we had missed while I was growing up and you were working full-time. So, on a rainy Thanksgiving Eve, I bundled you up and brought you to my home.

Four months later, five days before St. Patrick's Day, you died. You basically stopped eating and slowly wasted away. Nothing I could say or do made a difference. We argued regularly about diet and nutrition. I even stooped to the you-know-you-are-killing-yourself sermon.

You calmly responded that you didn't have a death wish. You just weren't hungry. At the time I didn't understand, but now I realize there is an intrinsic difference between a death wish and a will to live.

Now you are gone. I wish every day for the chance to call you, to talk about nothing, to argue about everything.

Were I not your daughter, I think I would have judged you a truly remarkable woman. Unfortunately, the characteristics that made you strong as a woman and successful as a career person are the same traits that put us in opposition as mother and daughter.

The perspective of your death allows me now to see that so clearly. It is also totally irrelevant. I just miss you and wanted to talk.

Love, Christy

—CHRISTINA M. ABT

*Christina lives in the beautiful hills of western New York. She is a freelance writer, creator of "Heart and Soul" newspaper column, and a Morgan horse breeder, and she works on renovating her old farmhouse. She is the mom of two grown children, who are always a part of her life. She remains her mother's daughter.*

# Awestruck Wonder

IT WAS THE TIME OF HARRY JAMES AND BETTY GRABLE, OF SEAMS IN LADIES' stockings, of Rosie the riveter, and of ration stamps for gasoline, shoes, fuel oil, sugar, and tires. It was a time of the 35-mile-per-hour speed limit to conserve fuel and tires. It was a time when all the church bells rang in all the little towns, beckoning all the people to come pray for the success of the Normandy invasion. It was a time when couples married hurriedly in order to steal a few days of married bliss before he went off to war.

Such was the marriage of Luther and Jenny.

They had dated all through high school in the little town of Miller, Missouri. She was a cheerleader, and he was captain of the basketball team. Both young people were known and loved by all the townspeople in their little community of six hundred.

Then Luther got his draft notice. They married quickly and rented a tiny house at the north end of town, near the end of the railroad spur that came from Mt. Vernon, the larger town eight miles to the south.

The townspeople watched Luther off on the train, and Jenny went back to the little house to wait for his return. Luther's letters to her came daily at first, then sporadically after he reached Europe, where he served as a bombardier on a B–17 bomber. Jenny carried his letters with her everywhere and read them not only to her friends but also to anyone in town who would listen, and everyone did. Jenny kept the little house clean, the lawn mowed, and the flower garden cultivated—all in anticipation of Luther's return.

The dreaded telegrams began to arrive: Will Johnson had been killed. Both of Perry Abiattia's hands had been blown off when he picked up a land mine. Herschel Sexton had been shot and had a plate in his head. Hershel's Purple Heart was sent to his wife, Dixie, who showed it to all the townspeople and wept over it.

Still, Jenny said Luther would come home safely—she knew it.

Two years went by. We little boys played our war games. We ran about holding our arms outstretched, making airplane noises and dropping imaginary bombs on imaginary targets. "I just bombed Hitler," one would say. "I just bombed Mussolini," another would shout. Then the war in Europe ended, and the letter arrived from Luther.

"My dearest Jenny," it said, "We will be ferrying our B–17s across the United States to California. I will ask my pilot to break formation and fly over Miller and your house. Be out front on April 3, at 10 A.M."

Now, none of us in that area had ever actually seen a B–17. Our exposure to that giant airplane had been limited to recruitment posters and movie newsreels. The word of the upcoming event flashed across Mt. Vernon, Aurora, Greenfield, Lockwood, and several other neighboring towns. On the appointed date, at least six thousand people had gathered in front of Jenny's house, many having parked their cars nearly two miles away. The people left a large opening in front of Jenny's house, where she stood awaiting the monumental event.

I was about seven years old then, as I stood holding onto my mother's hand, waiting.

We heard it long before we saw it. The roar of those giant engines built until it nearly deafened us. Then there it was—coming from the east just over the trees, nose high, flaps down, wheels down, bomb bay doors open, and huge propellers clawing the sky. It seemed to hang there, and yes! We could see Luther in the bomb bay waving at us!

The gigantic war machine banked to the left, flew around the water tower, and made another pass. That time Luther dropped a small supply parachute with a small box attached. It opened just a few feet in front of Jenny. Jenny ran to it, picked it up, and ran into the house. She later made a dress of the parachute—the camouflage type—and wore it proudly around town.

—JOE EDWARDS

*This scene took place over fifty years ago, and most of those who witnessed it are now dead. But Jenny and Luther's love for each other never died. Joe still sees them from time to time. He's collecting stories as amazing as this one from his hometown of Miller, Missouri, and writing a book of his memoirs.*

#  Mystery Man

EARLY IN THE MORNING OF AUGUST 1, 1975, I WOKE UP TO FIND MY HOUSE on fire with all seven of my children inside.

It was a big house with two bedrooms downstairs and three bedrooms upstairs. My two daughters shared a room on the main floor; my five sons slept upstairs. With very little time to spare, I ran upstairs to awaken the boys, then back down to get the girls. Three of the boys ran past me as I entered the girls' room. Two panicked and stayed upstairs.

I screamed to them, "Everything is on fire! But you can make it down the stairs and out the door if you hurry." Only one of my daughters ran out the door; I couldn't find the other one. When I found her and literally tossed her out the door, I thought I saw two figures go by me.

My home exploded behind me just as I left the porch. Once outside, I could only account for six of the children. I tried to head back in, but neighbors held me back.

I noticed a man, a stranger to me, talking calmly with my other children, who were sitting on a curb across from the burning house.

Soon after the fire department arrived, the last of my seven children came running around from the back of the house. After hugging him with relief, I collapsed on the curb and sobbed.

The man who had been calming the other children had left the scene. No one knew who he was, and I didn't think about him again until I went back into the building a few days later.

As I wandered through the charred ruins, I found some amazing things. The blaze had somehow spared one treasured possession, untouched by fire or heat, for each child. I even found one of my treasures: a little case with cards, stories, and mementos like the first lost tooth from each of my children.

Each item was something the kids had talked to the mystery man about.

I later learned that during his conversation with the children, he said he was sorry they were losing so much and asked what they would miss most.

Who was this man?

I never found out. I believe he was sent to protect us and the things most important to my children's innocent hearts.

—SUSAN STEVENS

*As horrendous as this tragedy was at the time for Susan and her family, you will learn from her other story in this book, "Angels Along the Way," that she and her children went on to become healthy and happy adults, and Susan not only survived, but thrived, in spite of this difficult experience.*

# The Face of God

In my years, I have seen the vastness of the Grand Canyon, the splendor of the Alps, the purple mountains' majesty of the Smoky Mountains of Tennessee, and the seeming endlessness of the Pacific Ocean. Yet, nothing I have seen, or ever expect to see, compares with what I once witnessed in a dark-paneled, antiseptic birthing room. Then and there, the power and love of God enveloped me.

I was on the last night of my clinical rotation as a nursing student on the labor and delivery floor, and I had yet to see a birth. When my children were born, fathers were relegated to the labor waiting room. Now, at 7:00 P.M. on my last student shift, my nursing instructor suggested I check into labor room four to see if I could watch the birth. With some trepidation, I knocked on the door, stuck in my head, and asked the young couple if I could possibly observe the birth of their baby. They gave me permission. I thanked them and found myself a spot in the room that kept me out of the way but still gave me a good view of the birth. Then I stood with my hands behind my back, studiously looking around the room at the preparations being made by the nurses.

The young mother, covered with blue sterile drapes, lay in the most uncomfortable and exposed position imaginable and was sweating profusely. Every minute or so, she would grimace, groan, and push with all her might. Her husband stood beside her, coaching her breathing and lovingly holding her hand. One nurse dabbed her forehead with a cool washcloth, while another encouraged her to rest when she could. The doctor worked on a low stool to ease the birth as best he could. I stood apart, proud of my unemotional, clinical detachment.

The nurse assisting the doctor said, "Here she comes!" I looked and was amazed at what I saw: the top of a head covered with black hair began to appear. I instantly lost the ability to call this wondrous occurrence something as medical as "crowning." Then the doctor began gently but firmly to turn the shoulders of the new life and pull. Transfixed to my spot, I am sure my mouth was agape. The doctor continued to turn and pull; the mother pushed; the husband encouraged; and an event that had taken nine long months of preparation was over in just a few seconds. At the sight of the infant's beautiful face, I felt such wonder that I truly believe angels sing at such times.

My professionalism and clinical detachment had deserted me, replaced with a warmth that surrounded me. At a loss for words—congratulations seemed such an empty and trite thing to say to these two blessed people at that moment—I nonetheless offered my congratulations anyway. After leaving the room, I walked around the corner into a deserted hallway and allowed my tears to flow.

That night some of my fellow students, all of whom were women and many of them mothers, asked me about the birth. Each time, I welled up again with tears and choked out that it was the most beautiful experience I had ever had. They would hug me or pat my shoulder, and with a gleam in their eyes say, "I know." Days passed before I could speak of the birth in any medical light. Even now, as I review that night, I continue to be in awe.

I have seen many sights in my life. Before my life is over, I will see many more. But none can ever compare to the night I saw the love, hope, and beauty of God in the face of a newborn child.

—Tony Collins

*Tony is a freelance inspirational writer, speaker, and a nurse. He writes inspirational stories for birthdays, births, and other special occasions. His wonderful wife, Pat, is his best friend. An English teacher and a writer herself, Pat helps and encourages Tony with his writing projects. An avid reader, Tony favors mysteries, inspirational books, and, of course, nursing and psychology books.*

# Gratitude

WHEN I WAS A SMALL GIRL, MY FAMILY AND I LIVED IN AACHEN, GERMANY. My dad owned a textile factory, and my mother kept busy raising my sister and me, playing tennis, doing charitable deeds, and taking an active part in Jewish community life. By 1935, anti-Semitism had become more pronounced, and bit by bit restrictions were imposed on us. Jewish attorneys were unable to charge for their services, and Jewish women could shop only in designated stores that offered inferior merchandise and food stuff. Doctors were no longer allowed to take care of the "inferior" race.

Jews were gradually forced to sell or close their businesses. We were unable to use public transportation. Jewish students were expelled from public schools. Everyone who could afford to, especially those in professional trades, left the country. However, some people felt that, although it was a difficult time, they had experienced hardship before, and life had gone on. Many Jews deluded themselves into thinking their families would remain safe. My father shared this false belief—after all, he had been, a decorated soldier in World War I. We hoped for an exit visa to the United States, but by the time we applied, thousands of requests were ahead of ours.

Denied schooling, I spent much time at home reading. As I sat with my books I became increasingly aware of a pain in my face that heightened to stabbing throbs. My face swelled up, and I was miserable. My mother concluded that I had a tooth infection, but she didn't know what to do. No one was willing to see a Jewish child.

In desperation, my dad talked to a nearby dentist, who finally agreed, for a hefty price, to look at me during the late night hours. Mom woke and dressed me, and the three of us walked to the dental office in the dark. Strapped into a chair, sobbing with pain, I tried to open my mouth as wide as possible.

I still remember hearing the dentist's dreaded words: "Yes, there is an infection. The second to the last tooth has to come out." Then he pulled and tugged and finally had to break the tooth.

While I squirmed in agony, my mother begged, "Can't you give her something for the pain?"

"No," he replied. "You Jews don't feel pain anyway. She's just acting up."

I don't remember much beyond that; I must have fainted. When I came to, my mother and father supported me as we walked back home. It was late, and no one saw us. The next morning I woke to blessed relief. The pain felt so much better, but strangely, the pillow was full of pus. As it turned out, the problem wasn't my tooth and never had been. I had a serious ear infection.

My mother made me swallow aspirins, placed hot compresses against my ear, and squirted warm oil into my ear canal. The infection finally cleared up, but it had unfortunately destroyed the hearing in my right ear. By the time my parents were able to send my cousin and me to nearby Holland to escape the Nazi menace and to get medical help, it was too late. The hearing has never returned to that ear.

Eventually, we came to the United States, and my family settled in Los Angeles. I attended school and college, always having to pay attention to where I sat, so I could hear. I later married and moved to Wyoming, and my husband, Edward, and I had four children—a girl, a boy, another girl, then another boy. Meanwhile, my hearing continued to deteriorate in both ears.

I finally gave up my stubbornness and decided to get a hearing aid. I scheduled an appointment at the University of Wyoming, which had a training program I had seen publicized in *Reader's Digest*. I didn't keep the appointment. That day, my younger son died as a result of an auto accident.

Another year passed, and I had to do something. Off we went to the university in Laramie, Wyoming, where they tried every hearing aid imaginable until they found one that helped me. After being fitted with the device, I recall walking around the campus and down a hall.

"What's that noise?" I asked.

"It's raining," my husband replied. I had forgotten the sound of raindrops hitting the ground.

When I became ill some years later, my hearing deteriorated further. So, I went back to the audiologist and got another hearing aid.

I've had a love/hate relationship with my hearing aids. Recently, I was walking with my dog, Tippi, along the shore of Fremont Lake, Wyoming, where we keep a trailer to use during the summer months. Because my hearing aid batteries were failing, I had turned them off. I was the only one walking on that windy, rainy day. I could feel the sand crunching under my feet and the droplets pelting my hair. I watched Tippi chase the waves crashing on the shore and a mother bird rising from the branches of a pine tree followed by four fledglings. Although I knew the birds were surely chirping, I couldn't hear them. I saw cars zipping along the nearby highway, spraying glistening drops into the air behind them. I knew they hummed as they glided over the wet pavement, but the sound couldn't penetrate my muffled hearing.

Suddenly, lightning struck the picnic area ahead of me with a crackle I could only sense. The thunder surely followed, although I could not hear its roar. Two deer ran into the clearing, hoofs pounding, spraying sand on the beach and rocks. They stopped and looked at me for a moment with wide, brown eyes, as startled as I was. Then they bounded over the bushes, crossed the road, and disappeared into the distance. As I watched the scenery unfold around me, my mind choreographed the sounds from my memory.

I regret the illness that took away my hearing. But as I walked along the lake that day, my heart filled with gratitude to God. For bringing my family safely out of Germany, when six million other Jews lost their lives. For my hearing aid—pain in the tochus (rear end) though it is. And for my sight, which allows me to see so much wonder.

Soaking wet, I returned to the trailer, where my husband waited. I replaced the batteries in my hearing aids and listened to him scold me for being out without my jacket and hood.

How good his scolding sounded to me!

—LIESEL SHINEBERG

*In November 1938, Liesel emigrated from Aachen, Germany, to Amsterdam, Holland, where she met a girl named Anne Frank, who became her playmate. Liesel's family immigrated to New York in 1940 and within a year moved to Los Angeles. She met her future husband on a blind date on a Monday evening. One month later, they married and moved to Wyoming, where her husband's family owned a business. That was forty-nine years ago, and they have lived in Rock Springs since. Liesel often speaks to schools, churches, colleges, and universities. She feels strongly that we must not forget the past, because that's how we learn to live the future.*

# In Dad We Trust

WHEN I WAS FIRST LEARNING HOW TO DRIVE AN AUTOMOBILE, MY FATHER would take me out for short rides around town. On one of these trips, my mother asked us to stops at the drugstore and pick up something for her. This involved parking, a new skill I was acquiring.

All the cars parked with their front ends facing the brick side of the drugstore. Huge cement stops in front of all the parking spots kept the cars a safe distance from the building. When we arrived at the drugstore, only one spot remained open, and it was between two parked cars. I pulled in with no problems.

My father asked me to pull up a little more, because the back end of the car was still in the street. I put my foot on the gas and pressed down, misjudging the pressure needed. The front wheels of the car flew over the cement block and stopped just short of the brick wall. I was terrified! With this my dad said, "Well, we have to get back over it, so put her in reverse and hit the gas hard." He never even raised an eyebrow.

Well, in Dad we trust, so I did it. Unfortunately, as we flew over in reverse, the wheel turned, and we scraped and damaged the side of the car next to us! To make matters worse, the car belonged to a good friend of my mom's.

I started crying and very nervously looked over at my father, who I was sure was going to kill me. He just looked at me and very calmly said, "Congratulations, now you're a real driver, Honey." He made me drive home, saying, "If you don't drive now, you'll never drive again."

I have never forgotten that moment thirty years ago.

—DEBORAH DOBSON

*Debbie is now the mother of three teenagers who are of driving age. She tried to incorporate her dad's attitude, love, and wisdom during driving lessons with her children, but it wasn't easy!*

# The Rainbow

JAN WAS THE TYPE OF FRIEND WHO COMES ALONG ONLY ONCE OR TWICE in a lifetime. We had been friends for twenty years, since nursing school. We were heart friends. Jan loved life, her husband, Rey, laughter, rainbows, and me.

We were both devastated when she was first diagnosed with cancer at age twenty-eight, thinking life had played a bad trick on her. After surgery three years later, the doctors pronounced her free of cancer. Within that time, she met and married Rey, the love of her life, and began a new and happy chapter in her life. Shortly after their marriage, the cancer returned with a vengeance.

Together they sought out the best medical treatment available at Mayo and Cleveland Clinics. For the next fifteen years she persevered through seven surgeries, three rounds of chemotherapy, and three rounds of radiation. Through it all, their love never faltered. She often speculated that God had sent Rey to her to see her through all of it. She would say, "I'd love to win the lottery to pay him back for being so good to me while I was sick." But she also knew no amount of money could equal the love they had between them.

The times Jan and I spent together were precious. We often talked about life and tried to understand, "Why all the suffering?" We would laugh together until we cried and cry together until we laughed. In preparation for her imminent death, Jan read 350 books on spirituality and healing. She and Rey read the entire Bible cover to cover, trying to find an answer to it all. She said she didn't want to be left out of heaven on a technicality!

I could see that Jan was losing ground the day I had to leave town on a business trip. I hated to go. I knew that she knew her time was brief. Three days later as I returned home in a blinding rainstorm, I began praying. As I prayed—alone in my van, just me and God—I became angry at God for not healing her as He did Job. For forty-five minutes I drove through the raging storm, ranting and raving, demanding an answer and crying out loud in my anguish as the lightning and thunder flashed and cracked around me.

Soon the storm subsided, along with my tears, and I drove out of the wooded area into a clearing. There, in the east, arched against a navy blue sky over a golden cornfield, was the most magnificent double rainbow I have ever seen in my life! I had to pull off the road and gaze upon it in awe. When I did, the most incredible thing happened. In an undeniable voice of authority and power, the Lord spoke to my heart. He said, "I have not forgotten Jan!" Goosebumps rolled down my spine, and I felt totally penitent and humbled. A sense of peace washed over me as I sat in amazement at the magnificent sight of the rainbows before me. Rainbows were Jan's favorite sight on Earth—other than, perhaps, the love of her life, Rey.

I knew there was more to this life than cancer could ever take away. I rushed home to phone Jan and tell her what had just occurred. Rey put her on the phone. I told her the Lord had revealed to me His promise and that He had heard her prayers. She said in a very weak voice, "Thanks for telling me about the rainbow. I love you, but I have to go."

Those were the last words I heard from my best buddy. She passed away the next morning. I miss her terribly, but she lives forever in my heart.

I wondered how Rey would do after Jan's death. He was always so self-sufficient, I knew he would get along okay but that it would take a while for him to get over her death. Rey said he would do it all again. He told me the peace, happiness, and total contentment he has experienced since Jan passed away are immeasurable. His comfort comes from knowing he did everything to the best of his ability while she was sick.

Rey still wears Jan's wedding band on his little finger. Inside the band is the inscription he had engraved when they got married, "Angel, my happiness is you."

—ROSE GORDON

*After Jan's death, Rey started a small organization; My Happiness Is You, that raises money for other cancer patients to help purchase something for their comfort or a vacation. He appreciates that he and Jan were able to take some memorable trips while she was feeling better. He also had angels made in her likeness to help raise money for the cause.*

# $\mathcal{H}$eart Muscles

MY HUSBAND AND I HAD A DILEMMA.

We had to move a 200-pound dining room table and two cabinets from our living room to the basement, and then move a heavy dining room table and two buffet cabinets up from the basement. We had no one to help us with the task. Everyone we thought of either had a bad back, was over the age of seventy, or was too busy to get hold of. You can't call a moving company for such a thing. The furniture stayed in our basement for weeks while we tried to think of a solution.

Then it dawned on me one morning when I went to the Lancaster County Health and Racquetball Club for my daily swim. As I walked through the place, I saw strong men everywhere! I approached Hoss, the resident repairman, explained my problem, and asked if he knew any big strong men who could come to our rescue. He immediately said, "I'm sure I can round up some guys for you." I gave him my phone number, went for my swim, and returned home. As I walked in my house, the phone rang. "Hoss here. I've got those guys for you. They'll be over this morning."

An hour later the doorbell rang, and I opened the door to find Hercules, Tarzan, and Rambo standing on my doorstep.

I just broke out laughing. Between them, those men sported 600 pounds of muscle, the most finely sculpted bodies I had ever seen close up! They could pick up our dining table with one hand and eat a sandwich at the same time. Hoss had done his job well!

The men saved the day for us. They moved all the furniture around as needed, joking the whole time as if it was the most fun they'd had in a long time. As they worked, we talked, and I got to know them a bit. Humphrey Seth Afari had won second place in the 170-pound weight class at the world championship power lifting competition. James Lewis, the "big guy" (they were all big, believe me!), had won the world champion masters competition in the 200- to 220-pound class and third place overall. He also had set a national record in his weight class by lifting 435 pounds. Eh—what's a dining room table? Jean Alexis, who was new to competition, had yet to win any trophies, but he looked like a winner to me.

Those heroic guys didn't come to my house because they were offered money. Since they usually slept after working out before heading to their third-shift jobs, they had also missed out on valuable sleep time. All three men came to my assistance simply because Hoss asked them to help a lady in distress.

Where I come from, we call these guys *mensches*. I take comfort in knowing that it's not out of style for nice guys to help a stranger.

Hoss, Humphrey, Jean, and James not only moved our furniture that morning, they moved my heart as well.

—AZRIELA JAFFE

*Azriela continues to swim at the health club every day, and whenever she runs into her new friends, she gets a big hug. They didn't move her furniture to get their names in a published book, but when she told them their story would be published, she got big smiles! Azriela knows who she'll be calling when she or her husband Stephen decide to move from Lancaster, PA, where they now reside: Hercules, Tarzan, and Rambo!*

# Who Am I?

ON THE WARM FOURTH OF JULY WEEKEND OF 1989, I HEADED OUT OF Portland to visit my eighty-eight-year-old dad, who was living in an adult foster care home. Dad had all the classic symptoms of Alzheimer's/senile dementia, and I had made the painful decision to place him in the home. I felt guilty about it. After all, this man had taken marvelous care of me for years.

His caretaker, Judith, and I were sitting in the living room when Judith said, "Your dad has really been talkative the last few days. He's been telling us about how he worked for the Union Pacific Railroad, married your mom, and then moved to Harrisburg, Illinois, and how he adopted you."

"Adopted?" I asked.

She must have noticed the astonished look on my face, because she said, "You didn't know?"

No, I didn't know. I was sixty-one years old and would have known if I was adopted. Wouldn't I? My wonderful mother, Ella Seeman Adams, who died eleven years ago, would have told me.

Wouldn't she? I left in a daze. When I got home, I told my husband about this revelation. He assured me it was the ramblings of a sick man who didn't know what he was talking about. I don't know why I didn't leave it at that.

I had to find out. I called a dear old friend of my mother's and simply asked her what she knew about my being adopted. There was dead silence on the other end of the phone line. Finally she uttered five words that put me in a tailspin: "How did you find out?"

Then all of a sudden it hit me. Who am I? For sixty-one years I had been Betty Estelle—the only child of two marvelous, caring parents. I had been raised a Protestant, even though Mom had been confirmed in the Jewish faith. Because we lived 120 miles from the nearest synagogue, Mom felt I should have some religious upbringing. It had become a funny family story that when the rabbi married Mom and Dad, he made them promise to raise their children in the Jewish faith, and for Dad to be circumcised. They did neither.

Now I learned that my ethnic background wasn't Jewish. After all, my family's medical history wasn't mine. My cousins and aunts and uncles weren't my blood relatives. I finally understood why I didn't look anything like any of my relatives.

Asking Dad questions didn't bring any answers. His physical and mental condition rapidly deteriorated until he died. The question "Who am I?" still ran through my mind, even though everyone told me to forget it and that, at sixty-one, I wasn't going to get any answers anyway.

But I did get an answer. I discovered the Boys and Girls Aid Society and they had my birth and adoption records. One afternoon a consultant sat with me and my husband to read some items from my file. She said, "I can't tell you the last name you were given, but you were given the names of Helen Marie, and you were born on your birth mother's birthday." My husband was astonished when I collapsed sobbing into a chair. He didn't understand. I had a name! The society offered to search for any current information on my birth family. However, given the age the birth mother would now be, I wasn't given a great deal of hope.

In January I received a phone call. "Are you sitting down?" the society helper asked. "We have found your birth mother. She is alive and well."

Three days later I got on a plane to San Diego to meet my mother. When I got off the plane, I saw nobody who looked as if they were looking for me. Then this small woman came through the crowd and looked me in the eye, and I knew this was the woman who had given me life—Tresa Kipp Delaney.

We celebrated our birthdays together here in Portland. I invited everyone, and they all came—even my half brother. I had a brother! I had nieces and nephews to add to the ones that were mine by marriage!

I had my children and grandchildren! I had a multitude of friends! There were 150 of us at that party.

My birth mother and I shared many visits, phone calls, and birthdays together. I treasure the little doll she gave me, because she said she had always wanted to buy me a doll for "our birthday." I cried with her when she told me the story of how she was forced to give me up for adoption when I was five weeks old. The morality of 1928 was far different for an unmarried mother than it is today. I was angry when I read the message her father had sent her sister. "Go to Portland, take your sister Tresa with you. She is besmirching the family name."

Tresa Kipp Delaney died in 1998.

I'm not sure when the burning question "Who Am I?" seemed to fade. I guess it was when I realized I had the best of two worlds—a mother who gave me life and a mother who gave me a life. The question of "Who Am I?" is no longer so important, because I have grown very comfortable with all the things that have made me who I am.

—BETTY BERGSTROM

*Betty lives in Portland, Oregon. She is a semi-retired 71-year-old widow who enjoys her children, grandchildren, and her new and old friends. She and the brother she found ten years ago also enjoy a relationship.*

# An Angel in Disguise

MY OLDEST DAUGHTER, AMBER'S, SOFTBALL TEAM WAS PLAYING AT THE California state championships. The tournament was held in the heart of a well-populated area with a major highway running the length of the whole south side. It was a city facility with four beautifully maintained diamonds and neatly cut grass all the way around the outside.

We arrived with a few minutes to spare and got situated at our vantage point of choice, behind the backstop, where we could see my daughter pitching for her team. During the short wait before the game began, I took in the wonderful sunshine and enjoyed the sights and sounds of the kids playing on the grass.

As I admired this beautiful setting, I noticed a man who was definitely out of place, sitting at the far southeast corner of the park, near the street. Given the wonderful weather, we typically saw several homeless people around our city. Although it was hot out, he had on one of those heavy, plaid winter jackets, buttoned to the top as if the temperature was 50 degrees. He also wore what seemed to be the dress-code pants of the California street person: Levi blue jeans, no longer blue.

Like many homeless people who hang out in parks, the over-dressed man carried all his earthly belongings in a single shopping cart, which he'd probably stolen from the local shopping center.

Then my daughter's team took their places to start the game, and I turned my attention back to the diamond, not wanting to miss a single pitch. If her team locked in one of the top places in the tournament, they would qualify for the nationals.

After several innings, there was enough of a break in the action for me to notice the homeless man getting up from his resting place and walking across the grass toward us. He was headed straight to the area where I stood. I tried to avoid eye contact with him and to make myself as invisible as possible. To my relief, he walked only as far as the drinking fountain. After he finished getting a drink of water, he lingered for a moment to watch the girls' game.

Many thoughts passed through my mind as I watched him. How old was he? Did he have children? How did he end up living on the streets? Still, I was relieved when he turned and walked back to his shopping cart without asking anyone for anything.

The day in the park continued, and my two sons, aged nine and three, started playing kickball on the grass around the perimeter of the ball field. By then, I was fully absorbed in the softball game; it was in the last regulation inning, and the two teams were tied.

As engrossed in the game as I was, I heard and can still remember my older son, Chase's, scream: "Erick, stop!" I instinctively turned my head toward my boys, and as if watching a movie in slow motion, I saw my younger son chasing after the ball his brother had kicked, running directly toward the highway. At mid-afternoon, the highway was loaded with fast-moving cars. I, too, screamed : "Erick, stop!" I began to run in his direction. I was about forty yards from the street. Erick's little legs were moving fast, and like a tiger running to take down an antelope for dinner, he was gaining on the ball. Just in the nick of time, the homeless man jumped up and ran in front of my son, then only a few feet from the highway.

The kick ball, like an antelope that escapes a pursuing lion, continued on, only to be bounced along down the street by several cars. A few second later, I reached my son and the man. How could I thank him enough? I reached into my pocket, pulled out all the money I had, and tried to give it to him, but he refused. With a shake of his head, he said, "That's okay, Man; I just wanted to help."

I again tried to give him the dollars in my outstretched hand. Now I was doing the begging.

"Please take the money," I pleaded. Reluctantly, he finally reached out and accepted my thank-you gift. Then he turned and, as he had earlier, without saying a word, walked back to the park bench he called home.

Just an hour earlier, I had tried to ignore him so he wouldn't ask me for any spare change. As he walked silently away, I realized I would gladly have given everything I had for his act of kindness. No longer was he a dirty, homeless man, living in the park with all he had in the world stuffed into a cart marked Lucky's. To me and my family, he was a big, beautiful guardian angel.

—DAVID SIMS

*David and Cindy Sims live in Southern California with their four children, Amber, Brystol, Chase, and Erick. David is a distributor of telecommunication and Internet products. Cindy is a homemaker and home-schools her children.*

# $\mathcal{J}$osh and Beau

JOSH, MY BUFF COCKER SPANIEL, WAS A GOOD PET TO ME FOR MANY YEARS. I adopted him from a pet store in 1984. He was my roommate when I was single and became my daughter, Heather's, protector when she was born in 1987. He was there for me when I needed a friend while going through a divorce in 1993. Through all the heartaches in my life, Josh always offered the comfort of his wet, cold nose.

In 1994, Josh moved with Heather and me to Albuquerque, New Mexico, where we started a new life. Josh died on the morning of September 27, 1995.

During the eight years Heather had grown up with Josh, she had grown very attached to him. After losing him, she wanted nothing more than to get another dog right away to replace the emptiness she felt. My boyfriend, Jerry, whom we were living with at the time (and who is now my husband), had two other dogs, but Heather did not think of them as "hers." However, I became pregnant with my son, Jerry III, and did not want the responsibility of another dog.

Heather, though, managed in her own way to get me to "just look" everywhere—in the newspaper and at pet stores—for a dog for her. She finally wore me down. One October day Heather and I went to the local dog pound just to "look around" and see what was there. We spotted a female buff cocker spaniel in the lost and found section that Heather instantly had to have.

Since the cocker was a stray, she was not adoptable until the mandatory amount of days had passed without her owner claiming her. We found out when she could be placed for adoption, if she remained unclaimed, and left.

On the Saturday the cocker spaniel was eligible for adoption, Heather and I returned to the dog pound before they were even open and waited in line. To Heather's joy and, I must admit, with much hesitation on my part, we adopted the cocker. Heather named her Beau. Before taking Heather's pup to her new home, we stopped at a dog groomer—Beau was a mess.

The following Monday morning, we took Beau to a vet for an examination, a requirement for any animal adopted from a dog pound. The vet informed us Beau not only had a hernia that required immediate surgery, she also had bad knees that soon would need replacing—procedures quoted at a very high price. Unable to handle the dog's medical needs at the time, I had no choice but to drive straight from the vet's back to the dog pound and return her.

Of course, leaving Beau at the pound broke Heather's heart. To my surprise, even I had become attached to Beau, and I cried with Heather that night. When we'd taken Beau to the pound, the workers had told us they would put her to sleep the next morning, because her medical conditions made her unadoptable. By returning Beau, we'd given her a death sentence.

In the middle of the night, in a moment of clarity—or maybe insanity—I called the dog pound. Of course it was closed, but someone answered the phone. I asked them not to put Beau down and to place a note on her cage saying we had changed our minds and would come back first thing the next morning to get her. Although I had no idea how we'd manage it, I knew it was the right thing to do, not just for Heather, but for me and for Beau.

The next day, Heather and I were again waiting at the dog pound before it opened. We took Beau home with us and made her a permanent part of our family. We immediately scheduled the hernia surgery, but she developed another hernia from the surgery and had to undergo another operation. After owning Beau for about a month, another dog attacked her, which damaged her eye so badly she had to have her left eye removed and the lids sewn shut.

I have never regretted my decision to go back to the dog pound to rescue Beau. We may need to replace her knees someday, but we'll cross that bridge when we come to it. Beau has been with us for almost four years, and I hope she'll be with us for many more.

Someday, Heather will have to endure the loss of Beau, the way that I did Josh, and I'm sure it will be very difficult for her. I also know that the experience of finding, saving, and loving Beau has opened Heather's heart—and all of our hearts.

—DEBBIE CARTER

*Debbie resides in Albuquerque, New Mexico, where she holds the full-time job of taking care of her husband, Jerry; three children, Heather, Jerry III, and Rachel; and three dogs.*

# Kassidy

I HAVE WORKED WITH YOUNG CHILDREN MOST OF MY ADULT LIFE. HAVING no children of my own, my career provides an outlet through which I can guide and nurture. I currently work with a program in Southeast Oklahoma designed to meet the needs of American Indian children with disabilities.

In November 1995, we were notified that a special needs child was about to enroll in our school. Before the child's mother came in to enroll her, we curiously looked over her application. Her name was "Kassidy." She was three years old and a double leg amputee from spinal meningitis. She also was reportedly missing several of her fingers.

When her mother arrived to do the required enrollment paperwork, we cautiously asked her where Kassidy was. She informed us she had left the little girl in the car with a friend, because they had not brought along her "legs."

The mother, who was single, clearly wore the weight of the world on her shoulders. She explained that, while Kassidy was very excited about coming to school, she was apprehensive. She shared stories of Kassidy's previous experiences with groups of children at day care centers, of how she was shunned and isolated, because the children wouldn't play with her. We encouraged her to bring in Kassidy and show her around her new school.

I was not prepared for the incredible spirit of this beautiful, smiling child who clung to her mother, her little knees wrapped tightly around the mom's waist. Her mother set her on the floor, and she took off to explore, running on her knees. That week's curriculum was dinosaurs, and her face lit up as she went from classroom to classroom, telling all she knew on the subject.

When they left, I called the director of the program and explained, "I have to have this child!" Even though my classroom was full, I wanted her in it.

The next day during learning time, I excitedly told all the boys and girls about Kassidy. She began the next day, and they loved and accepted her, because I did.

A few weeks later, during an art project, Kassidy watched as we took off each of the children's shoes and traced their feet on a piece of paper. The children squirmed and giggled when the pencil went around their toes.

When Kassidy's turn came, she insisted we pull off her shoes too. It was a difficult task to get her shoes off, but I did it. I stood her on the paper and started to trace around her perfect little plastic feet. When I started around the toes, she started to giggle wildly. I have never heard anything more beautiful and at the same time more heartbreaking.

Kassidy taught me more about handling adversity and about laughing under the most unbearable conditions than I, the teacher, taught her during those two years.

—CORRINA HYDE

*Kassidy remained in Corrina's classroom the next year and became best friends with a little girl named Carissa, who has cerebral palsy. Kassidy is now in second grade, and Carissa is in first grade; they attend separate schools. Corrina, who wants to keep in touch with Kassidy "forever," continues to provide both girls with the opportunity to get together at her house about once a month. This summer, Kassidy went to Disney World through the Make a Wish Foundation.*

# 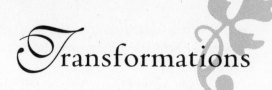Transformations

A FRIEND OF MINE DECIDED TO END HER SKIN CARE AND MAKEUP SALES business and to return all the unused products. Her sample cases, however, were not returnable. After much thought about how best to utilize them, she contacted a local retirement home to offer a free demonstration without the end-of-party sales pitch. My friend invited me to help.

We arrived at the retirement home with two sample cases and a shopping bag full of wash cloths, cotton balls, makeup mirrors, cotton swabs, and boxes of tissues. The activities director showed us to a recreation room conveniently equipped with a large round table, good lighting, and a functioning sink. We unpacked our supplies, as aides gathered our guests for the party.

One by one, five ladies came in and sat around the table. Three of the women were in wheelchairs and two used walkers. All were white haired, shriveled, hunched—mere skeletal beings. Ranging in age from seventy-nine to ninety-one, the ladies greeted us pleasantly and, with heads bowed and hands folded in laps, thanked us for giving them something different to do. They seemed very old and totally resigned to the blandness of themselves and their lives. My soul cringed.

I acted as assistant, handing out samples of cleansing cream, warm wash cloths, and then moisturizers. The ladies remarked how pleasant the creams felt on their faces and how soft it left their skin. As they chatted, I realized they were not as drab and old on the inside as they were on the outside. Rather than consider them fragile grannies, I decided to relate to them as I would my girlfriends.

Two were legally blind, and the others had minimal vision. We offered them the choice to forgo the makeup demonstration. Without exception, they wanted the makeup and asked us to apply it. Happy to comply, my friend dabbed on face powder; I followed with an eyebrow pencil. As I stroked soft sienna where brows used to be, I raved about their radiantly glowing skin and teased about how sexy they would look after their "celebrity" make-overs. I asked, "Who wants daytime eye shadow, and who wants sultry evening eyes?" All hands went up for the sultry, sexy look! They were definitely getting into it, and I obliged with touches of brown shadow.

Finally it was time for lipstick. Every head turned up, presenting dainty shrunken lips to receive the muted red color. Those who still had vision wrestled with makeup mirrors, trying to see themselves. The activities director and aides "oohed" and "aahed" over how lovely they looked. When I called them "gorgeous temptresses," each one sat a little taller, beaming. A camera appeared, courtesy of the activities director, and the ladies were thrilled to oblige, each requesting an eight-by-ten! They had individual photos taken and then several group shots, to guarantee at least one shot would be good enough to post on the dining room bulletin board.

As I watched the photo shoot, I thrilled at their transformation. Yes, the touches of makeup gave them renewed color, but something else, something mystical, had happened. Now animated, the "old ladies" planned their lunch-time assault on the dining room, asked the aides to help them change into "prettier" dresses, and joked about flirting with this or that man. They had become vibrant women again, alive with the joy of their sexuality once more. They had been given the gift of feeling young again, even if only for an afternoon.

—LYNNE DAROFF

*Lynne's friend moved away shortly afterward, leaving her to pursue other rewarding volunteer experiences, including a recent stint teaching citizenship to elderly immigrants.*

# $\mathcal{S}$he Lied

When I was young, after we ran away from my father, my brother and I lived with my mother in a travel trailer. Then, even more so than now, some people looked down upon you for living in a trailer.

The trailer was eight feet wide and about thirty feet long. Mom and I slept together in a twin bed in the middle; my brother slept on the couch in the living room. In the winter, we layered newspapers between our thin blankets and lit an oil heater. Our toilet was often frozen when we awoke in the morning. We walked to school, almost three miles. I remember Mom coming to find us once, while we were walking home during a blizzard. I lost a pretty scarf my uncle Harry had given me that I was wearing that day. I didn't have another one.

Because we had only a five-gallon water heater, every night I heated extra water on the stove so I could wash my hair. We also caught rain water in a barrel to rinse our hair and massaged an egg into it to give it shine. We planted morning glories around the trailer, and they swirled up their strings and blossomed magnificently around our tiny home.

Vegetable fields surrounded us, so after the harvesters had picked, we would sneak out and gather the remains. On good days, we had plenty of tomatoes or asparagus.

One evening Mom fixed a bit of rice and chili and split it between my brother and me. When we sat to eat at the tiny folding table, I asked her why she wasn't eating. Looking right at me, she calmly said she'd eaten as she cooked.

Even in my youth I knew she had lied and that lying was wrong, but I also thought she was very brave for lying and going hungry. That incident has always stayed close to me.

Once Mom and I were invited to a wedding. Only I went. My aunt and uncle took me with them, and I wore the only dress my mother owned. It was too big, but I felt very important wearing it. I was asked to dance, and I was sure it was because I looked so fetching in that royal blue dress.

Twice a year we went to the hardware store and purchased a tin of flax soap. We mixed it in a bucket with hot water and scrubbed our trailer from top to bottom, leaving behind its wonderful scent. Mom always said that, even though we didn't have much money, we could still be clean and spotless. I never went to school without an ironed and starched blouse, and my brother never went without a laundered white shirt.

My mom lives with me now. She has numerous health problems, and when we first brought her into our home, she couldn't walk and could barely talk. She tires easily, is on oxygen all the time, and has a new valve in her heart.

People think it is a burden for me to care for my mother. Well, life can be tough, but my mother taught me to see the wonderful things in life—like morning glories and the smell of flax soap.

—WANITA BATES

*Wanita currently works and teaches at a community college in central Florida. She is active with her church's youth group and is the president of the soccer booster club of her son's high school. She has been happily married for twenty-eight years to her best friend, Richard.*

*Due to emphysema and heart disease, Naomi is quite limited in her physical activities, but Wanita takes her to swim class twice a week. They share in each other's lives and grow morning glories on the trellis surrounding their back door.*

# Christmas Angel

THANKS TO MY CONSERVATIVE JEWISH BACKGROUND, I DID NOT BELIEVE in angels. That is, not until Christmas Eve of 1979, when an angel brought unexpected joy to my home.

As often happens in divorce, my five- and eleven-year-old daughters not only lost the security of an intact family, they also tearfully left behind neighborhood friends, a familiar school, and the comfortable amenities of a large house. These had all been replaced with a cramped two-bedroom apartment in a poorer part of town.

I arranged to take my vacation during my children's winter school holiday. We spent evenings planning an ambitious itinerary of activities: cookie baking, matinees, arts and crafts, games, a pizza night, and evening car rides to view neighborhood holiday lights and lawn displays. The anticipation worked its magic, and their spirits seemed to brighten.

The week before the school break, however, devastating news of multiple family disasters arrived faster than we could process the pain, clouding our vacation plans. By Christmas Eve, gloom enveloped our home. An afternoon outing to a movie did little to improve our mood.

Upon returning to our apartment, we were astonished to see a majestic, six-foot Christmas tree aglitter with metallic icicle strands propped against our front door. In mute wonder, we looked back and forth, from the tree to one another and around the deserted street. Excitement built, and the girls begged to keep the orphaned tree.

"Maybe it's for us," insisted my older daughter.

"Yeah," echoed my younger child. "I bet an angel brought it to us!"

I laughed aloud at the idea of an angel bringing a Christmas tree to a Jewish family. Caught up in their newfound elation, I pronounced the tree "ours."

We dragged it inside and headed out to the only supermarket in our small town open that late on Christmas Eve. With holiday merchandise marked down to half price, I gave a nod of approval to a tree stand, two boxes of multicolored balls, a package of six Santa figurines, a 100-foot string of miniature lights, and one lone paper angel.

Back home, we maneuvered "our" tree into a place of honor in our tiny living room. The girls snipped and glued and painted paper decorations. With an exhilaration that had been absent for months, we strung the lights, placed the paper angel on top, and festooned the tree with store-bought and homemade ornaments.

Finally, with a girl snuggled in each of my arms, we sat in semi-darkness, mesmerized by twinkling Christmas tree lights. Smiles and contented sighs proclaimed the end of our long emotional crises; there was joy in our new home. I sat in thankful amazement that a Christmas tree had the power to uplift Jewish spirits. My five-year-old softly whispered, "Do you really think an angel brought us this tree?" All I could do was answer honestly from my heart. "Yes," I whispered, holding them closer, "I'm sure of it."

The annual winter vacation became a family tradition, complete with a "Jewish Angel" tree in remembrance of our heaven-sent gift. For seventeen more years, we held our breath and felt the familiar tingles up our arms when we placed the original paper angel atop each tree.

Now my adult daughters have their own homes. There are no more luxuriant vacation days spent together; there are no more Jewish Angel trees. Still, every Christmas Eve, my children phone to sigh and reminisce about our angel and about the special childhood memories intertwined in the branches of a six-foot tree. For all these years, I also have held onto that paper angel from our first Christmas tree.

—LYNNE DAROFF

*The worn paper angel now sits on Lynne's desk as a daily reminder to watch in times of great sadness for the miracle that will surely come.*

# An Old Chipped Bowl

MANY YEARS AGO, WHEN MY FIRSTBORN WAS AN INFANT, WE CALLED A horrendous apartment in a former storefront building our home.

We'd been there for some time before I realized a wizened old lady lived in the ground-floor apartment behind us. She rarely went outside—perhaps because the winter was long and harsh. But she didn't go onto her sun-warmed porch even in summer. She had no relatives, lived on her Social Security benefits, and was very unfriendly.

My son suffered with colic until he was old enough to eat solid foods, and everyone near the poor little tyke suffered right along with him. He seldom slept for more than two hours at a stretch, and his distressed cries pierced the quiet nights. Nothing helped much—except time!

I began to worry that my neighbor was lying awake nights and possibly thinking my husband and I were torturing our poor little infant. So one morning, with the baby tucked under one arm, I rapped on her door. When she finally responded, I haltingly apologized for disturbing her sleep as I handed her a plate of fresh-baked cookies.

She said little but eyed the baby with interest through her thick glasses. I rattled on nervously. Finally she said, touching his chin tentatively, "He'll outgrow it all right."

We did not exactly become friends, but I took to visiting her more frequently, usually with some "extra" homemade soup or other offering. Now and then she'd ask me to get her something at the grocery store across the street or the nearby drugstore. She never invited me inside her humble quarters. However, the day I mentioned to her that we'd finally found a house of our own to rent, I thought she looked more sad than usual.

Soon we were packing cartons in preparation for our move. Our house was only two miles distant, so it was a relatively easy transition. My husband borrowed a friend's truck and made a few trips, while I tended the baby and swept the floors one last time. When my husband returned for the last of our belongings and his family, we said a grateful good-bye to the apartment, happy to be moving on to a more homey place.

When I climbed in the truck beside my husband, I had to push aside a tissue-wrapped object on the seat of the truck, but I didn't think much about it. When we arrived at our new home, my husband came inside with me, saying, "I brought in whatever this is."

"Whatever this is" turned out to be a lovely cut-glass bowl with a chip in its fluted rim. On a torn bit of lined paper in the nest of the bowl was a note that read, "I've lost a dear neighbor. Good luck, Mrs. W."

After the move, when my husband and I went to the center of the village to stock up on groceries, I'd rap on Mrs. W.'s door. Sometimes she responded, and occasionally I'd run an errand for her. She remained fairly uncommunicative, but I noticed she always seemed glad to see my growing son.

A year or so went by in much the same way. Then one day I knocked on her door with a small loaf of homemade bread in hand, and a business owner from next door paused in his sidewalk sweeping.

He inquired, "You didn't hear? The meter reader found poor old Mrs. W. dead a couple of weeks ago."

There'd been no funeral, no obituary notice in the local paper. There was little to mark her last years. I went home and wept into the sparkling chipped bowl.

—JANET "NETT" HOUNSELL

*Janet Hounsell, a retired newspaper photo/journalist, still writes and studies people like the sad lady of The Chipped Bowl story. She says she has no interest in gardening but cultivates a sense of humor. Lately, she's been telling her family that when the time comes, she's lobbying for a coed nursing home with reliable computer hook-up, though she's in no hurry to move.*

# When a Camper Goes "No Mail"

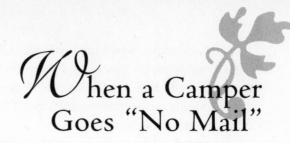

PAUL IS THE YOUNGEST OF FOUR AND OUR ONLY SON. EVERY DAY I THANK God for our "surprise." He almost always wears a smile on his face, and he is my best hugger. Not a day goes by without two or three bear hugs from him.

Despite his gentle manner and open affection for family members, Paul has never been a "homebody." His first sentence told me he wouldn't be. I was upstairs making the bed when I looked out the window and saw him toddling toward the neighbor's yard. I had thought he was in his playpen in the family room.

"Paul!" I yelled frantically from the upstairs window.

He looked up and said cheerfully, "Bye! I go for walk!"

As he was growing up, I learned the best way to motivate him was to promise he could visit a friend or invite some friends over. He'd rather do something with friends than receive toys, money, television time, or any other kind of reward.

He often talked eagerly about going to camp with friends, but it seemed that every summer, family and sports activities prevented it.

But last fall he and his best friend made plans in earnest, and nothing came up to prevent them from going. The day they had been longing for finally arrived. My husband was working, so Paul and I shared the forty-five-minute ride with Dustin and his family.

"I'll write you soon," I said after hugging him in Cabin 1. He didn't give me his usual bear hug. He just stood there.

"No, don't write me. I want to be alone."

I was floored. I searched his tanned face and deep blue eyes for some explanation. All I could see was that he wanted me to leave.

"You don't want any letters?"

"Well, if Dad dies, write me."

What somber, unsettling parting words, I thought. On the drive home I shared my sadness with Dustin's parents.

"You didn't hug him in front of the other boys, did you?" asked Fred, a former scoutmaster.

I had seen about six boys perched on a bunk on the other side of the cabin, but at the time I didn't think they were watching. Now I understood why Fred and Cathie had exited the cabin with just a quick wave to Dustin.

When I got home I told Catherine her younger brother had gone "no mail."

"Why would he want letters? It's only a week," said Catherine, who has never been to camp.

"Wouldn't you want letters?"

"Well, you could send them if you wanted to. But I wouldn't want you to expect me to write back."

How did I comply with Paul's "no mail" request?

He was flooded with letters. I wrote dozens in my head, but only sent one by mail. The rest were prayers addressed to God. I prayed for his physical protection. I prayed he would keep his gentle and affectionate ways. I prayed he wouldn't grow up and away from us too fast.

When we picked up Paul on Friday night, his huge grin said it all. He had a great week and a week's worth of dirt on him to prove it.

My letters on wings were more helpful than anything I could have sent with a postage stamp.

After his bath, he sneaked up and gave me the best bear hug ever.

—GRACE WITWER HOUSHOLDER

*Journalist and author of* The Funny Things Kids Say, *Grace Witwer Housholder lives in Kendallville, Indiana. She still gets hugs every day from Paul.*

# Broken Legs

ONE TIME A GENTLEMAN CAME TO THE ORPHANAGE WHERE I LIVED WHEN I was eight to teach the children how to do woodworking.

I remember the night I finished my first project. It was a small table with a Formica top. I was so proud of that table, and I looked upon it as though I had created a life. It was the first time in our whole lives that the orphanage had allowed us to use our minds.

I could hardly wait to give my little table to Mother Winters, our head mistress, as a gift.

Because the table legs were not dry from the clear coating we had applied, the instructor asked us to wait until our next session before taking our projects to our dormitories. But I was just so excited and happy I couldn't wait.

I moved my table toward the doorway and waited for the right opportunity to escape. Then I went out the door like a flash, running through the darkness with my little hands underneath the table top, smiling from ear to ear, as I headed toward the dormitory.

When I got there, I placed the beautiful little table beside my bed and stood there for about ten minutes just looking at what I had created. Then Mother Winters entered the room. I pointed at the table, and she smiled at me. I felt so proud. She asked me where the other children were, and I told her they were cleaning up the sawdust and would be coming soon. She walked over to the table and ran her hand across the slick Formica top. "It is very pretty," she told me.

When she touched the table leg, she noticed the leg was still wet from the newly applied clear coating . She asked me why I had brought the table into the dormitory with the legs still wet. I didn't know what to say, so I just stood there with my head down and said nothing.

"Were you supposed to bring this home?" she asked.

"No ma'am," I told her.

Mother Winters walked over to the little table and kicked it over onto its top. Then she stepped onto each of the small table legs, breaking them off. She opened the side door and ordered me to throw the little table out into the yard.

After Mother Winters left the building and all the other children were asleep, I opened the outside door and went out to get my little table. There was sand stuck all over the legs. I brushed and cried, and brushed and cried, but the sand would not come off.

I hid the table in my closet and never returned to the wood shop after that.

The following year I gave the little table and legs to Mother Henderson, my houseparent, so she could throw them away.

About thirty years later, I tracked down as many of the orphanage children as possible for a reunion. That's when I learned where Mother Henderson was living. Several weeks afterward, I drove up to see her, and we talked for four or five hours.

As I prepared to leave, she asked me to come down to her basement and help her get something important. So we climbed down into her dark, cold, damp cellar.

The shaking seventy-five-year-old woman walked over into a dark corner and picked up something. As she turned around, I could see she was holding a little table with four broken legs.

"Do you remember this?" she said.

I just stood there with my head down, not saying a word. I couldn't speak for fear of crying.

"Roger, I want you to have this."

Mother Henderson gave me back the table I had given up for lost so long ago. She had kept it all those years, never knowing whether she would ever see me again. She decided to save the table, because she couldn't rid herself of the pain she remembered seeing in the eyes of the orphan who had made it.

The inscription of my name was still etched on the bottom of the table.

Since then, I have sanded, clear coated, and replaced those broken legs.

That little Formica table—my first woodworking project so many years ago—now sits in my granddaughter Chelsey's bedroom, only a few feet from where I sit now.

—ROGER DEAN KISER, SR.

*Roger grew up in an orphanage in Jacksonville, Florida, until he was thirteen years old. He went on to a civilian military career and is presently on disability. Roger's goal is to reform orphanages and to stop them from treating children like prisoners.*

# More than a Roll of Quarters

TEARS STREAMED DOWN MY CHEEKS AS THEY ROLLED MY DAY-OLD daughter out of neonatal intensive care. Rachel had been born with a genetic defect that caused her esophagus to connect her stomach to her trachea rather than to her throat. Although, as a full-term baby, she looked perfectly healthy, she could not swallow food.

The surgeon reassured us surgery could repair the malformation, but he also reminded us it was a serious procedure. Because she was an infant, he anticipated needing to take out one of her ribs just to create the space required to reach into her chest and do the repairs. The surgery would affect both her digestive and pulmonary systems. Because of the anesthesia, she would require a ventilator. There would be numerous opportunities for infections.

Within hours of her birth, our daughter had been transported to a large research medical school hospital for the surgery. My wife was so drained from the delivery and the shocking news that she decided to stay where the birth had occurred, near our home. Because my wife was still in a different hospital, I thought I would have to face the surgery by myself.

But I didn't face it alone, after all. Two friends from church came to be with me. One, Terry, was an incredibly busy man who worked on Capitol Hill as a technical advisor to one of the House of Representative subcommittees.

Terry stayed until the surgery was over and the doctor reported things had gone well. He had to return to work, but he said he wanted to help and slipped something into my hand. As he left he said, "I know how hard it can be to find change to make phone calls."

He had placed a roll of quarters into my hand, communicating an enormous thoughtfulness. Out of his busy schedule, Terry had taken the time to go to a bank and purchase a roll of quarters. He thought ahead about the situation and did more than just leave me with the usual words, "If I can do anything, just call me." Terry had anticipated one of my needs and met it without my having to ask.

When I see the scars on my daughter, I am thankful for that life-saving surgery. I am also thankful for a true friend who was there in time of need and showed me how important the practical expressions of love can be. Thoughtfulness is so valuable. May God help us all to consider one another.

—JOHN KING

*Today Rachel is a healthy eleven-year-old, who plays on a soccer team, which her proud parents coach. John continues to work as a minister. Their family moved about seven years ago, so he has much less contact with his friend Terry than he would like.*

# $\mathcal{S}$old It for Scrap

WHILE WATCHING TELEVISION RECENTLY, A FORD TAURUS COMMERCIAL got my attention. It was about a young boy who is involved in a car accident and calls home to tell his parents he's sorry about the damage to the car. The father tells the boy, as long as he's okay, not to worry about the car.

The commercial reminded me of my brother Eli.

Back in 1980, Eli was a drug addict. After he used drugs in front of my kids (I allowed no drugs in my house), I kicked him out and didn't speak with him for ten years.

In 1990, he ended up in jail for most of the year. When he got out, he was clean and drug-free and returned to Georgia. I was leery of him being around my children. However, he was family, and my mom asked me to at least be civil toward him. So I was.

I introduced him to the missionaries from my church and, sur- prisingly, within two weeks he became a member of my church. From that point on, he was the brother I remembered from my teen years—honest, hard-working, and always thoughtful of others.

My dad cherished a Gold Wing motorcycle he owned. One day, my brother needed a way to work and begged my dad to let him use the Gold Wing. Reluctantly, my dad agreed, but adding the phrase, "If you damage my motorcycle, you better not come back!"

Eli never came back.

On his way home from work that night, a motorist hit and killed my brother. The day after Eli died, my dad and I went to pick up the motorcycle from the police impound lot. We couldn't believe our eyes. The motorcycle had received only a few minor scrapes. My dad said something then that made me realize just how much he loved his children, even though he never said the words I love you. He said, "I would rather have my son back than this motorcycle."

My dad sold the motorcycle for scrap two days after the funeral. He has not been on a motorcycle since.

After not speaking to my brother for ten years, I had been allowed only one year with him to make up for all the years I had missed. Eli died exactly one year after joining my church.

Since then, I have tried to live by the motto "Forgive and forget." I never told my brother I forgave him. I hope he knows that now.

—KATHY GRIMES

*Kathy now lives in Valdosta, Georgia, where she and her daughter Debbie are attending college. She works for the Alcohol and Other Drug Education Office at the university she attends. In addition to writing short stories, Kathy is currently writing a play and a novel. Her brother Eli left behind a wife, four sisters, and two brothers, as well as his parents.*

# Typesetter's Apron

THE WEEKLY NEWSPAPER IN NEW HAMPSHIRE WHERE I WORKED IN THE 1970s was an equal opportunity employer. That is, even if you were a so-called photo–journalist like me, you could very well get the opportunity to sweep the floor before a high-profile candidate came to do his handshaking bit. If someone on the paste-up desk was sick, you might also get to paint out tiny dots on negatives of entire broadsheet pages.

This last chore was likely to involve "all hands," especially if the antiquated presses broke down, making it impossible to get the weekly edition "put to bed" on schedule.

I had stayed home until my children were somewhat self-sufficient. When I took the job at the paper, I needed professional clothes that would serve me whether I was covering a fire or an awards dinner. Creating a new professional wardrobe had been expensive, so you can imagine my frustration when, week after week, smeared ink grime ruined one work outfit after another.

As if the job and the small town didn't have enough unusual characters, there was something else peculiar about the place. The newspaper passed from one owner to another with an unusual clause in the sales contract: Willy, a fifty-year-old man who lived on the third floor of the building, was part of the package!

Willy wasn't quite right in the head. Each new owner had to find ways to persuade him to stoke the furnace, shovel snow, wash the windows now and then, clean the toilets, and otherwise earn his keep. He was a grouser and complainer, and no one had known him to ever do a thoughtful thing for someone else.

So, everyone was flabbergasted when Willy took the initiative to find out how and where to buy a typesetter's apron and purchased one out of his own money—not for himself, but for me!

I'll never forget his puffed-up chest and how I felt when he presented it to me—wrapped in newspaper, of course! I was stunned and moved to tears. I praised him enthusiastically for his kindness, not just on that day, but for days and weeks afterwards. Willy's one simple act of kindness restored my faith in human nature.

A marvelous transformation then took place. Willy became a new man—someone who looked for ways to help his coworkers and to earn their admiration. This gruff man who had appeared so mean-spirited turned out to be a lonely man who just needed some positive attention.

When Willy reached out to me and then to my coworkers, we reached back, and a sweet, loving man emerged.

—JANET "NETT" HOUNSELL

*Now retired, Janet still writes, and her credits (other than* Heartwarmers*) include a 200,000-word town history written for her local historical society. Willy died on the job, quite suddenly, a few years after Janet left the newspaper, so she never had a chance to tell him how much he taught her. This is her opportunity—perhaps he is reading this from wherever he is.*

# Something About Harvey

I ADVISED MY MOM, WHO WAS SEVENTY-ONE AND NO LONGER ABLE TO care for a young dog, to adopt an older dog. "How about getting a small dog?" I suggested.

No, it had to be a great dane. She would consider no other breed. Within a few short months, Mom had lost her fourteen-year-old great dane, Kirby; her husband, Mike; and her sister, Mickey—and she was very depressed. I thought a new dog to love would really help.

Then one day, there he was. She had bought a year-old, ninety-pound great dane puppy. He was *huge*. I called him the "house horse." She named him Harvey Wallbanger, because his tail whacked everything in sight, so much so that the tip was a bloody mess. Blood also splattered on the walls, curtains, bed, furniture, and our clothes. We walked around with sponges, constantly wiping off Harvey's blood. We tried everything to bandage his tail, to no avail. We all had bruises from getting whacked by it. That tail was a weapon.

We fell in love. Harvey had a new home.

He was in poor condition when we got him. He suffered from worms, an ear infection, malnutrition, and bowel problems. We spent a small fortune on his health problems. Then we had to get him fixed. We had to continuously clean up after his accidents—and when a great dane has an accident, he doesn't mess around. It didn't matter. We adored him.

Harvey was also an escape artist. We dropped a bundle of money on collars, harnesses, and tie-out chains—all of which were just stop-gap measures while we built a tall fence to contain him. No matter what we tried, he got loose within minutes. We had to stand outside and watch him closely. If we looked away for a minute, he darted away (though he always returned in about twenty minutes). Once, he ate the doorknobs right off the door and then took off. He could open the sliding glass door even when it was locked. Although he was pretty aggravating, we loved him anyway.

Whenever we left him alone, Harvey tore up the trash and everything else, leaving us with huge messes to clean up when we came home. Remember, this dog has a very large mouth: he can carry a VCR in his mouth, no problem. He was so destructive, we could rarely leave the house, and I dubbed him "destructo dog." I spent hours cleaning up myriad pieces of whatever he had chewed up that day. God, that dog was frustrating.

But we couldn't help loving Harvey—and he loved us too.

He liked to put his enormous mouth gently around the upper part of your arm, where he would leave plenty of slobber and bits of dog food, usually after drinking out of the toilet. It was his rather gross way of saying, "Play with me!" His considerable bulk and weight didn't stop him from trying to sit on your lap or lying on top of you in bed at 3:00 A.M.

He drove us nuts. But there was just something about Harvey. We loved him.

Then came the fateful day when he slipped out of his collar and got loose again,. The police came to our door with bad news: A car had hit Harvey, fracturing his skull. We rushed him to the emergency vet hospital, assuming we would have to put him to sleep, but the doctors thought there was hope. We told them to do everything they could to save him. After several days went by, he seemed to improve and came out of the coma. He knew us. We were so hopeful. We made plans to hire a nurse for him until he recovered, knowing it be a long, expensive ordeal. We didn't care about the cost. We loved him.

I prayed about every five minutes, "Please God, we've lost so much recently. Don't take Harvey; he's just a baby. Please give him another chance at life." The Bible says to pray and to then believe your prayer has already come true. I visualized Harvey, fully recovered, going for walks with me. I went to the vet hospital every day to sit with him and encourage him to fight for his life.

There was something about Harvey. Everyone at the vet hospital fell in love with him. Even in a coma, he inspired good will in people. The veterinary staff doted on him and called in on their days off to check on his progress. I entertained them with funny stories about Harvey. We all became close in our quest to save him. They wanted him to live as badly as I did.

On the tenth day he took a turn for the worse. Although he still acted happy to see me, he seemed to be losing his ability to fight. I had a very bad feeling. The next morning, I knew he wasn't going to make it. As I waited for the vet to arrive and concur, I felt my heart breaking, but I knew I had to be strong for Harvey. I had to let him go.

When the vet arrived, everyone seemed to know. They all began to gather around to say good-bye to Harvey and to comfort me. Everyone—the technicians, the receptionists, and the vet—joined us in loving Harvey, crying, and comforting each other. I marveled that one big, black-and-white, unconscious dog had so affected people who dealt with the death and suffering of animals every day.

There was just something about Harvey. I now understand what it was: He gave us unconditional love—and we loved him back unconditionally.

—KIM VORBAU

*Harvey's people are Nona G. Biss and Kim E. Vorbau. They reside in central Ohio. Nona is a retired bartender, and Kim is a geologist.*

# $\mathcal{G}$ino's Haircut

RECENTLY I WENT TO GINO, MY HAIRDRESSER OF TWENTY YEARS, AND spoke the words he thought he'd never hear: "Cut my hair short." It had been over thirty years since I'd worn my hair much shorter than shoulder length.

As the first four inches dropped to the salon floor with a silent thud, I momentarily regretted my decision. But as the hair mound deepened, my head felt freer and my shoulders lighter. I decided that even if I ended up looking like an Irish pixie, losing my locks was liberating. I loved it.

The first stop after my shearing was to visit my friend Bonnie, who was in the process of living with and dying from cancer. She had just withdrawn from active treatment of her disease and signed on with hospice.

That day we talked at length about death—hers, mine, and the world's. She said she wasn't afraid to die, and believed death was a wonderful thing. She reasoned that we humans don't know this, because if we did, we'd all commit suicide! I'm still not sure whether she was joking or revealing one of life's great secrets!

Bonnie loved my haircut. She also wore her hair in a short style. She needed a trim, but didn't have the strength to get out of bed, much less to a hair salon. In a flash, I volunteered Gino.

Now, as I said, Gino had cut my hair for over twenty years. I wouldn't have said, however, that we were good friends or that I had the right to commit him to a haircut without consulting him. Nonetheless, I had. Now I prayed he would agree.

I left a message on Gino's answering machine, explaining Bonnie's illness and the circumstances of the haircut. I used my most persuasive Irish pleading, prodding tone and hoped for the best. For three days, I heard nothing. Disaster! I'd made a promise to a dear friend, and now I couldn't deliver. I tried to imagine how to call Bonnie and tell her.

That night, however, I received a message of salvation. Gino called to say he would be pleased to cut Bonnie's hair at her home. Relief and gratitude swept over me, along with a bittersweet feeling. Something told me the haircut would be Bonnie's last.

Gino visited Bonnie the next day, as promised, and gave her the haircut she badly needed. She called to thank me for her new "do." She loved it. Her phone call was followed by one from Gino, expressing gratitude for introducing him to Bonnie. He considered it an honor to fulfill her haircut request. It was one of those treasured moments of human interaction and compassion that happen so infrequently in our jam-packed lives.

Four days later Bonnie died. It was a gentle passing, surrounded by those who loved her most.

In retrospect, that one simple act of getting my hair cut triggered a series of occurrences that affected the lives of Bonnie, Gino, and me. It was nothing earth shattering. Society as a whole didn't change. But it taught us that our individual actions do affect others and that we are not alone in either the struggles or celebrations of our lives.

Knowing Bonnie, I wouldn't be surprised if that was her intent from the start.

—CHRISTINA ABT

*Christina is a freelance writer and creator of the "Heart and Soul" newspaper column. She lives on a farm in the rolling hills of Western New York, where she breeds and raises world champion Morgan horses. Friendship and kindness are a daily part of her life there.*

#  Still Waters

FOUR YEARS AGO ON ONE OF THOSE NONDESCRIPT DAYS—NOT TOO HOT, not too cold—I arrived at my destination, unaware of the drive or much of anything other than seeing a few cars in the parking lot. Still, I remember that day as clearly as I do the days President Kennedy was shot and the shuttle *Challenger* exploded on takeoff. I lingered awhile and listened to one of eight special songs I had copied earlier that week for a ceremony.

I opened my car door and tried to compose myself before I went into the building. I had come to pick up a package. I don't know what I had expected, but as they handed it to me I thought it was too small. The clerk handed me a clipboard and said, "Could you please sign here?" He gave me the receipt and a sheet of instructions.

I placed the package in the trunk, so my wife wouldn't see it in the car. The tiny bundle lay next to some leftover programs and dried flowers I had put there before, in preparation. My brother-in-law, a commercial fisherman here in California, had reminded me several times not to forget the flowers for the boat ride he had arranged for the following morning.

The next morning came very quickly. My brother-in-law asked if we could arrive at his boat around 5:00 A.M., because the trip we were taking would take more than two hours. It was still dark when we arrived at the dock, where my father and a family friend, who were invited along for the trip, were already waiting. My wife, Cindy, had declined to go with us; she wanted to stay home with our three children.

As streams of light appeared in the east, we all boarded, and the boat engine roared to life. I handed my dad the package and the dried flowers, and I jumped over the rail onto the deck.

We pulled out from between the docks and headed toward the mouth of the harbor. I expected rough seas when we hit the open area just outside the harbor, but I saw only still water, the bow of the boat making the only visible waves. A gray, high-level overcast filled the sky.

We proceeded with a slow chug toward our destination, the lighthouse high on the hill overlooking the point of the peninsula. I prayed I would be able to do what needed to be done. When we reached the lighthouse, my brother-in-law turned the boat due west. I went up onto the captain's deck to watch the rings on the sonar system scroll away from the peninsula point—one mile, then two, and finally three miles west of the lighthouse. Then it was time to complete the task for which we had journeyed out into the Pacific that morning. My brother-in-law cut the engine and circled the boat to keep our position.

I went down to the main deck where my father and friend had stayed during the whole trip. My dad held the package; my friend held the flowers. I asked for the package, which was wrapped in plain paper with a single name written on the side: "Derek." I opened the paper to reveal a purple bag that contained a plastic box with a lid on one end. I pulled out the box, removed the tape holding the lid, and looked inside. There, for the first time, I saw the ashes of my two-year-old son, Derek, who had drowned in our pool a week earlier.

I then moved to the back rail of the boat and asked my dad to pray. My friend gently dropped the flowers into the motionless water. As my dad concluded the prayer, I slowly poured the contents of the box over the side. A whitish-gray cloud formed a funnel shape down into the dark depths of the ocean. At that moment the most beautiful site I've ever seen broke the eerie calm. From the northeast came a pod of twelve dolphins, young and old, jumping through the surface of the water in joyous celebration. Above us, as if in the perfect style of a military fly-by for a distinguished officer, ten pelicans flew past just a few feet off the glassy surface.

All week I had prayed God would show me how to make this tragedy a celebration of my young son's life. Through His beautiful creatures and perfect timing, God brought it all together.

Two years later, we continued to hurt from the loss of our son, and still we longed for the joy a two-year-old could bring to our family. Cindy prayed that if there was any way God could provide a child for us to love, He would fill a special place in our hearts.

That Sunday at church I noticed a child whom I'd not seen before. He was around the age of two and was very possessive of the toys in the playground. When I inquired about him, I found he was the child of a young mother who had been unable to properly care for his needs after her husband had left. He was living with his uncle and aunt, who also were young and had a six-month-old son of their own. They were seriously considering returning him to his mother. I wondered aloud to his uncle what his plight would be if he went back to his mother. He informed me she would most likely send him to live with his grandfather in Guatemala. At the time, Guatemala was in deep turmoil. I couldn't bear the thought of this child being sent to live in such chaos without me doing something. I asked his uncle to please contact the mother and have her call me.

I had lived in a state of numbness since we had put Derek to rest. Nothing I had previously considered important—my executive position, friends, sports, or even, sadly, my family, held any luster. I had a hard time focusing on anything other than the empty feeling in my life.

The child's mother did call, and we talked for a long time. I was very nervous and excited about the possibility of working out the details and adding a new addition to our family.

On a cool Thursday night, two years of prayer were answered when Erick came to live with us as our son.

Although I hadn't been looking for a replacement for the son I'd lost, Erick came into our lives at the right time. The numbness still lingers somewhat, but the emptiness in my heart has been replaced with a joyful two-year-old named Erick.

Whenever I feel the uneasiness and sorrow building up inside, I hug our newest gift from God, and a feeling of calm, like warm still water, restores me.

—DAVID SIMS

*David's family remains strong now, a few years after Derek's passing. Erick has grown into a very special member of their family. When Cindy and David started their family, they decided to name their children in alphabetical order—Amber, Brystol, Chase, Derek, and then Erick. It's amazing how God works.*

# $\mathcal{L}$ast of the Flour

WHEN I WAS GROWING UP IN THE OIL FIELDS OF OKLAHOMA IN THE 1930s, our dad worked for a refining company. We lived about two miles from a small town, but Dad worked close to the main store. So Mother would tell Dad all the groceries and things he needed to bring home after work.

She made big breakfasts for all us kids with some left over for two or three hungry dogs that belonged to one kid or the other. I guess you could say we were farmers, because Mother always tried to grow a big vegetable garden. Dad planted corn and potatoes. We had a cow, sometimes pigs, and always chickens.

Those big, big breakfasts of Mother's always included big pans of hot biscuits right out of the wood stove. When the flour reached the point of, say, half a batch of biscuits, Mother would say, "Oren, that is the last of the flour." Dad would say, "Is that all?" Then she might think of a few other things we needed.

With much snorting and fidgeting, he'd dig in the front pocket of his overalls for his stub of a pencil and hunt for a piece of paper (sometimes a hunk of brown paper bag). Then Dad would wet the point of the pencil in his mouth and begin the list. The first item was flour, of course. Then my folks conversed back and forth over the list—while all the time we continued eating breakfast. Then Dad would put the stub of the pencil and the list in his overall pocket, where it remained all day.

We anxiously waited for Dad to return, because we usually got a bag of penny candy when he went to the store after work.

They were married for sixty-one years. After Dad died, Mother lived on alone. Now and then a grandchild lived with her for a while, and we were always close by, seeing to her needs.

Now she can no longer live alone, which brings me to the "last of the flour."

While clearing out her things and removing items from her kitchen for the last time, I found a canister about half full of flour. So I decided to use the "last of the flour."

This is how it went . . .

With part of the "last of the flour," I baked a big peach cobbler with peaches from trees my mother had planted. The cobbler was made for the funeral celebration of a very dear friend who was special to Mom and Dad.

The second thing I made from the "last of the flour" was a pumpkin pie for a potluck dinner at the church where Mom and Dad had worshipped.

I used the last of the "last of the flour" to make a chicken pot pie for their grandchildren and great-grandchild, which would have pleased Mom and Dad.

That's the "last of the flour!"

She will be with us, her kids, to the end—when she goes to join Dad.

—OPAL MARTIN JAYNE

*Opal was born in the Kiamichi Mountains of Oklahoma in 1920. She is the first of ten children born to Oren and Lavonia Martin. She has three children, five grandchildren, and two great-grandchildren. Opal and her husband, Robert Jayne, have been married fifty-six years. She loves God and has been a Sunday School teacher for thirty years.*

# Old-Fashioned Perfect Love

I VIVIDLY REMEMBER, AS A YOUNG BOY IN EIGHTH GRADE, PRAYING TO God to bring a Christian girlfriend into my life. I didn't have to wait long before the matchmaking God had planned even before I was born was put into effect.

In November of my freshman year at Clinton High School, a gorgeous-looking senior girl named Kristi Conway stopped me in the hall. The name Powers emblazoned the back of my shirt, and she asked me if I was John Powers' brother.

I stammered, "Yes I am."

"Do you think you could give me his address at college, so I could write him?"

"I would be more than happy to do that," I croaked.

I was immediately love-struck.

Later that day, while a teammate and I shot baskets in the gym before practice officially started, the woman of my dreams walked out of the locker room. I couldn't take my eyes off her. Then she looked at me and smiled. It wasn't just any smile; her smile lit up the whole gym and made my heart beat faster.

I was in love, and all was well with the world. Suddenly I felt as if I had been stuck with Cupid's arrow.

It hurt. In fact, as intense pain coursed through my cranium and the ground rose sharply up to meet me, I wondered why Cupid had shot me in the head. The sound of a certain senior girl's laughter rang in my ears as she exited the gym.

While I was staring at my future wife, my buddy had thrown the ball to me. The ball had struck me in the head and knocked me off my feet. I thought the relationship had ended before it had even started, but it proved to be a good conversation starter the next time I saw her.

We started out as friends and began to write letters back and forth in study hall. Then we found out we were both born-again Christians, which gave us even more common ground. I knew she was the woman for me, but I was a freshman and she was a senior. She would be going off to college. So I prepared myself for the end.

Our friendship grew through letters and three-hour phone conversations. I will always remember the first time I spent more than an hour talking on the phone with her. I had always thought people who talked on the phone for more than two minutes were dorks with no life. All of my phone conversations until that point in my life consisted of: "Hey Mike, you want to play baseball today?" "I'm there dude!" Click.

With Kristi, I learned why people spent an hour on the phone. Our friendship blossomed into something more through the hundreds of letters we wrote one another. We saved them and still have them today in a drawer.

I remember the first time I held hands with her. We were sitting on the couch at my house, watching television with my little brother and sister. I don't remember how our hands got stuck together, but man oh man, the fireworks went off overhead! I was actually holding her hand!!

Six months after we started going out, I kissed her for the first time. She went to kiss me on the cheek, and I turned my lips to hers before she knew what was happening. Hallelujah!

Kristi decided to work that summer and when Fall came she didn't go to college. For the next three years, she coped with dating someone who was still in high school, while she was out in the "real world." I grew to love my future wife more and more each week.

As Christmas of my senior year approached I knew it was time to get her a ring and ask her to marry me. I purchased the ring, and then came the hard part—asking her dad's permission to marry her.

I went over to her house on a Sunday to watch football with her dad on what became the longest afternoon of my life. I wasn't about to bother him while the game was on, so I had to wait for a commercial. But every time a commercial came on, my heart would start beating wildly in my chest and my breath would get short. By the time I had worked up enough nerve to ask him, the game would come back on. This went on for perhaps an hour and a half.

Finally I got off the couch, knelt next to him, and fumbled with my shoelaces like I had to tie them or something. My heart felt like it was going to leap out of my chest and flop around the room.

He waited about a minute before he said, "Mike, is there something I can do for you?"

There I was on my knees in front of Kristi's dad, looking up at him like some lost puppy.

"I ah . . . I would . . . ah . . .

"I-would-like-to-marry-your-daughter-if-that-is-okay-with-you. I-bought-a-ring-already-and-want-to-give-it-to-her. Some-guys-at-work-had-been-asking-her-about-a-ring. I-love-your-daughter-and-would-take-care-of-her . . . ."

My mouth was running a hundred miles an hour, and I couldn't stop talking.

He looked down at me and said he would like that. Then he patted me on the head. After I fetched his newspaper and slippers, I was able to enjoy the rest of the afternoon.

I wanted to give her the ring on the land my dad owned by Turtle Creek near Carver's Rock. Kristi and I loved it there, and I planned to take a moonlight stroll near the river with my future wife and our two dogs. Well, my older brother got wind of my master plan about an hour before I put it into action.

"You're going to give her the ring where!? You don't give a woman her engagement ring by a creek!" he yelled.

I had thought it would be perfect, but I had never done this before.

He told me I should take her to a nice restaurant and give her the ring over dinner. He placed $50 in my hands, made reservations for me at a restaurant, and shoved me out the door.

When the meal arrived and the waitress left, all we had left to do was pray before we started to eat. It was our practice to hold hands while we prayed, so I reached my hands under the table and slipped the ring box into her outstretched fingers. Her eyes lit up. I will always remember the look on her face when she opened the box and saw the ring. "Kristi Conway, will you marry me?" I asked.

"Yes!" she said.

On our wedding day, I sang a song to Kristi entitled, *I Would Never Promise You*. I still remember the words by heart:

I would never promise you with just my strength alone,
But all my life I'd care for you and love you as my own.
I've never seen the future. I only see today.
Words that last a lifetime would be more than I could say.
This love inside my heart today is more than mine alone.
It never changes. Never fails. And never seeks its own.
And by the God who gives it and who lives in me and you.

I swear these words I speak today are words I'm gonna' do.
So I stand before you now for all to hear and see.
And promise you in Jesus' name a love he's given me.
Through the years on Earth and as eternity goes by,
The life and love he's given us are never going to die.

The greatest gift we gave to one another on our wedding night was the gift of ourselves. We had both waited to have sex until we got married. We were able to look into each other's eyes that night in the hotel room and say to each other, "I saved myself totally for you."

Nowadays, coming into marriage a virgin is no longer fashionable. It is a decision I am proud of and that gave us great joy. Kristi was my first love, and I hers. Together, with our love of God, we share a bond that will never be broken.

—MICHAEL T. POWERS

*Michael has been married to his sweetheart for over ten years, and he reports that she still makes his heart go wild when her smile lights up the room.*

# $\mathcal{A}$ Tiny Miracle

ONE WARM DAY BACK IN THE EARLY 1980S, WHEN MY CHILDREN WERE STILL children, I took my three children and a neighbor girl over to my in-laws home in Grand Prairie, Texas. After checking in on my mother-in-law and letting the children visit with their grandparents, we began our return trip to Irving along Hunter Ferrell Road.

Hunter Ferrell is an old road. When I first came to the Dallas area in the '60s, it was still a gravel road, which they later simply spread blacktop over. It has two ninety-degree turns about one-half mile apart. We had the windows down and were having a wonderful time, singing at the top of our lungs, enjoying the day and one another. We had just gone through the first ninety-degree turn and were about halfway to the next sharp curve, when a honeybee flew into the car and landed between my legs on the car seat. I was wearing shorts.

Bees and wasps had frightened me since my brother almost died from a wasp sting when he was young. I have learned to give these insects my utmost respect and as much clearance as possible. So, I immediately pulled over to the side of the road and tried to shoo the bee out of the car without it stinging anyone.

About that time a car came around the ninety-degree turn in front of us, traveling very fast and out of control and sliding sideways. I estimated the car was going 45 to 50 miles per hour into the curve—a dangerous spot where the posted speed limit is 15 miles per hour.

If it were not for that honeybee and my decision to pull over to the side of the road, the speeding car would have crashed right into us. God only knows what would have happened to my children and me.

At five months old, I survived an auto accident in which I flew through the car's windshield and landed fifteen to twenty feet away on a gravel road. I carry the reminder of that childhood accident on my face and legs. One fourth of my lip was sewn inside my mouth, and one side of my nose grows down a little more than the other side.

One such horrific accident in a lifetime is plenty for any person to handle. I guess God knew that.

I believe God gave us a miracle that day—a tiny miracle in the form of a honeybee that saved at least five lives.

—NELLIE SUE

*Nellie and her husband still live in the Dallas area. With their children now grown, they look forward to retirement and grandparenting. Nellie no longer fears bees and wasps, and she is now grateful for their existence.*

# A Perfect Little Number

WHEN CATHIE HENDERSON JOINED THE U.S. ARMY NURSE CORPS IN 1967, the Vietnam War was at its peak. The Army offered to pay for her last year in college. She also hoped that joining would give her a chance to displace her brother, who, as a Navy corpsman, might be at more risk than she would be in the combat zone.

I am Cathie's kid brother, the recipient of this incredible act of love.

As fate would have it, my sister got stationed at the 24th Evac Hospital at Long Binh on the head and spinal cord injury ward, just up the road from me. We often went into the local villages "Medcapping" (Medical Civilian Assistance Program). We both felt we had to find a good side to the wretched war. Surely there was more to Vietnam than the heartbreak of dying, maiming, and destruction.

During Cathie's tour of duty, she learned exactly how different combat nursing was from the New York City hospital wards where she had practiced as a student nurse.

When a severely wounded soldier learned Cathie was returning to the states soon, he asked her to call his mom when she got home.

Cathie kept her promise, and one of the first things she did was call his mother.

She was stunned when the mother began to sob hysterically. Only days before the soldier's mom had received a telegram informing her that her son had been mortally wounded.

"Not only is he alive, but he was well enough to give me your phone number, ma'am," Cathie told her. The shaken, but grateful, mother had her niece drive her to Cathie's house, so she could personally thank her for calling and taking care of her son.

That was the last thank you Cathie received for fifteen years.

When the Vietnam Wall in Washington, DC, was dedicated to honor the war's more than fifty thousand fallen veterans, Cathie felt it would be fitting to also honor the nurses and women who had served. Had it not been for the nurses, surely the Wall would have been bigger. No one knew better than Cathie that Vietnam was more than a "man's war."

A mysterious turn of events subsequently took place. Although the incidents defy explanation, they somehow lend credence to the bond that exists among those who served in that fateful war—a bond that can never be broken.

Cathie was attending a nursing convention to gather signatures and support for a memorial to honor the women who served during the Vietnam conflict. She displayed a bronze model of a proposed statue and talked with anyone interested in the memorial project. Hearing her voice, a man in the vicinity walked over and listened intently.

He introduced himself to Cathie and explained he had been injured in Vietnam, sustaining a severe head injury that had left him temporarily blind. He went on to say that he distinctly remembered the kindness of an Army nurse who had cared for him. He couldn't see her at that time, but he recalled asking her to describe for him the dress she was going to wear to her farewell party that evening.

"She told me it was a yellow dress with small white flowers. . . ."

". . . that I had gotten from the Spiegel catalog," Cathie finished his sentence for him, "a perfect little combat zone number!"

In the massive convention hall, they hugged and cried, marveling at the miracle of finding one another again, among the hundreds of thousands attending the convention.

After being medevaced to the states, he had regained his vision and become a nurse himself. His attendance at the convention to check out nursing job opportunities had brought them—him and Cathie—full circle to a very surprising and heartwarming reunion.

—TIMOTHY P. HENDERSON

*Cathie Henderson–Solomonson lives in Virginia. She has grown sons and a granddaughter. Still active in Vietnam veterans' affairs, she helped to establish the Vietnam Women's Memorial located near the Wall.*

*Timothy Henderson is a playwright and environmental activist. He and his wife, Rebecca, are raising their five-year-old grandson, Charlie, who is a constant source of warmth to their hearts.*

# Give Him All That You Have

IN 1995, AFTER A HEARTBREAKING DIVORCE AND MONTHS OF GRIEVING, my life revolved around an endless circle of empty days with nothing to do except cry and feel sorry for myself. Concerned about me, friends and family suggested I find a job to get my mind off myself. After fighting every suggestion, I decided maybe I did need to find an outlet.

I lived in an apartment in town, right across the street from a coffee shop. Wearing my long face, I went to the coffee shop every morning for breakfast and was greeted with a warm smile. The waitress always tried to make my morning as pleasant as possible. One morning, she told me they needed waitresses and asked me to come work there.

It had been years since I had worked as a waitress, but the idea of a job that would keep me so busy I wouldn't have time to think of my heartache appealed to me. My finances were in terrible shape, and I actually needed the job. So, I took the waitress up on her offer and reported for work the next day.

I worked second shift. Business was very slow, so customers and tips were few and far between. One afternoon, the door opened and a very nice-looking young man came in and sat down. I greeted him and proceeded to place a clean napkin and silverware before him. I asked what I could get for him, and he said, "A glass of water is all I need. Would that be possible, please?"

I said, "Certainly, sir," and gave him a large glass of water. He smiled cheerfully with a gleam in his bright blue eyes.

There were many days when I really didn't know how I was going to make ends meet. On that particular day I needed for the cafe to be busy, because I had to pay a bill. However, by the time the young man had come in at 5:00 in the afternoon, I had only made $3.25 in tips all day.

The man began to talk to me about his situation. He had lost his job and had nowhere to live. Now, he was homeless and living in his truck.

I asked him, "How do you take baths? You look so nice and clean."

"Oh, here and there I have a friend or two," he said.

"How do you keep that wonderful smile through all of this?" I wondered.

He told me, "Well, I could frown, but that would only get me down."

I poured him a cup of coffee, and he said, "No, I can't pay for that." I told him it was on the house. As I walked away, a small voice within my head said, "Give him the money you have." I was shocked. What did these voices mean? I needed what I had. But the voice and the feeling were strong. So I went to my purse and got the two dollars, reached in my pocket and got my $3.25 tip money, wrapped the money in a napkin, and walked back to the young man. I laid the napkin beside his coffee cup and said, "You have a nice day."

After he left, the customers started pouring into the coffee shop. Tips came from every direction, and when I left that night, I had cups full of money. When I got to my apartment, I sat down in the middle of the floor and emptied my cups of money. By 5 P.M., I had made only $3.25 in tips; at 11:30 P.M., I was in the middle of my living room floor, counting $63.50.

That day was a turning point for me. How could I have been so stupid as to waste almost two years of my life grieving over a lost love? How could I not realize that all the while there had been more love and concern for me to look forward to? Slowly, with each day that passed, I cried a little less, knowing I wasn't the only one hurting.

It has been nine years since the day I learned that life can be good and that God was there for me all the time; I just didn't know it.

—ANITA WISE

*Anita recovered from her heartbreak and returned to college. She graduated in May of 1999 with a certificate in Technical Illustration and Mechanical Drafting and is presently seeking employment in her new career. A talented artist, she hopes to create her own line of Christian T-shirts.*

# My Guardian Angel, Kim

IN 1978, I LEFT MY HUSBAND AND WITH MY FOUR-YEAR-OLD DAUGHTER IN tow moved from Baton Rouge to a very small town just across the Mississippi River. A friend of mine told me that I just had to meet a girl who was a city police dispatcher, because we were so much alike.

I did meet Kim and instantly began what was to become the closest friendship of my life. Within one month of meeting Kim, my daughter and I moved in with her. That's when she told me she was expecting a child. Eight months later, she delivered a beautiful baby girl. Our friendship grew even stronger, and Kim and I became inseparable. We looked and dressed alike; we even finished each other's sentences. It was quite eerie at times.

I have severe asthma, and Kim rushed me to the ER quite often and sat up with me on many nights. When the apartment next door became available, my daughter and I moved into it to give us all more room. We always wished we could knock out a wall to adjoin our apartments.

One day, Kim started limping. Soon after, a doctor diagnosed arthritis in her hip.

Kim's hip condition worsened over the course of the next year, and I advised her to get a second opinion. The new physician immediately sent her to Shand's Hospital in Florida, where surgeons removed a tumor from her hip the size of a five-inch cantaloupe. A few weeks later, the doctors had to amputate her leg.

Within months, she complained of back pains; and we soon discovered the cancer had moved to her lungs. As her health rapidly declined, I visited every day after work. One Tuesday, she didn't look very well, so I reassured her I'd visit early on Wednesday.

That morning, my asthma flared up, and I went into respiratory arrest. I was put on a ventilator and admitted to the hospital. After a week in the intensive care unit, I was released and wanted to go straight to Kim's house for a visit, knowing she was probably wondering where I was. Her family and mine decided that, because Kim was dying, seeing her would aggravate my condition. So, they kept making up excuses like, "She's sleeping," or "You have to rest." Four days after I left the hospital, on Saturday, March 4, 1989, my best friend, at the age of thirty-one, passed away without me having a chance to say good-bye.

Three months after Kim's death, I was back in the hospital on a ventilator. Every once in a while, I motioned to my mom that I wanted to write something. The only word I wrote was "Kim." Mom made excuses, saying that Kim was working or that it wasn't visiting hours. She didn't want to worsen my condition by reminding me that Kim had died.

Days later, when I went off life support, my mom said, "I didn't know what to tell you when you asked for Kim." It was then that I told her, "You don't understand. I wasn't asking for Kim; I was trying to tell you she was there in the room with me."

Kim always stood at the foot of my bed, smiling and reassuring me that I'd be okay, because she had "connections."

"After all," she said, "Someone has to stay behind to take care of our girls."

I have one very special guardian angel, and her name is Kim.

—KATHIE GUIDRY

*As the godmother of Kim's daughter, Brandi, Kathie has shared the responsibility of raising her with Brandi's grandmother, her legal guardian. Brandi is twenty now and lives on her own in the same trailer her mom died in just a few blocks from Kathie. Kathie and Brandi remain extremely close and see each other almost every day.*

# He Rescued Me

IN 1990, I WAS SEPARATED FROM MY HUSBAND, JOBLESS, AND FACING THE prospect of losing my home, because I couldn't pay my mortgage. On my way home one evening, as I stopped at the intersection of two rural roads, a little black-and-white dog came up out of the ditch and stood right in front of my truck. He peered at me intently, reminding me of the James Herriot short story about abandoned dogs and their heartbreaking efforts to find the people who so callously dumped them. I drove on, but a minute later, circled back and picked him up.

Victor Charles, as I named him, had been beaten and was starving and dirty. His eyes were red from road dust, and he was exhausted from his efforts to find his owners. A bath made him look a little better, but he was so malnourished, he could only keep food in his stomach when he was medicated.

His inner wounds were even worse. He feared all men. Every time I reached to open a cupboard door, he ducked down as though apprehending a blow. When I took him to the vet, he cowered away from the open door of the truck, obviously terrified of riding in it. To him, a ride no doubt meant being dumped in the country again.

Things weren't going much better for me at the time. The pain of the divorce, fear of the future, fruitless job searches, and just plain despair often overwhelmed me. It frequently seemed like too much to bear, and more than once I thought of ending my life. But there was always Vic. Who would take care of such a badly damaged little dog if I didn't? Even in the depths of my depression, I knew I couldn't put him through another abandonment. So, I continued to live—for him.

Nine years later, Vic and I have a much different life. He is happy and healthy. Medication controls the epilepsy that the vet thinks the beatings he sustained earlier in his life caused. To look at him now, you'd never think he'd known a bad day!

Our story reminds me of the line at the end of the movie, *Pretty Woman:* I rescued Vic, and he "rescued me right back."

—Lisa Bartel

*Lisa now has a dream job and a wonderful new husband who pledged in his wedding vows to take care of Vic and their other animals. Lisa's husband and Vic adore one another. The couple also has a precious infant daughter, Nora Kathleen. Vic turned ten on August 21, the eighth anniversary of the day Lisa found him.*

# Angels Along the Way

MY HEART SANK AS I SAT ACROSS THE STREET FROM THE BURNING building and stared at the flames leaping in the darkness. Tears rolled down my face as I realized our "new beginning" wasn't starting out the way I had planned.

It had taken me so long to gather the courage to move my seven children and me 100 miles away from a physically, emotionally, and verbally abusive husband. There, I hoped we would find a better life. I'd bought the house a month earlier, and we'd been allowed to move in while it was going through escrow. Nine more hours, and I would have been in the local attorney's office signing all the final papers. Instead, I stood and watched as the house and my hopes burned.

My thirteen-year-old son, Jim, ran down the dark country road to my best friend, Patsy's, trailer. Jerry, Patsy's husband, took us all back to the trailer. After getting the kids settled down in makeshift beds on the floor, I collapsed on the couch. I lay there in the dark, smelling the acrid smoke that filled the room and wondering what was next. Where would we go?

The next day we set up camping gear in the yard next to Patsy's trailer. I tried to get help through the local welfare office, but they wouldn't help unless I had a place to live. I spent the subsequent two or three months trying to find someone who would let me move in—which was not easy with seven children—so I could then apply for help. To make matters worse, after our home burned down, the local towns-people started gossiping that we had done it ourselves.

We hit one bad patch after another. My ex-husband wouldn't help; he didn't even pay child support. Two of my children ended up in the hos-pital—one with pneumonia and another with ear infections so severe one of her eardrums had punctured. When I asked her why she never told me how badly she felt and how much pain she was in, she said she knew I had enough to worry about. Again, my tears flowed. My children deserved more than they were getting, and I couldn't even give them the basics.

Just before Halloween, a neighbor of Patsy's offered us the use of a very small trailer with two large rooms built onto the side of it. I gladly accepted. It was small and cramped, but it was somewhere to live, and I could then get help from the state. It had a wood-burning stove, and I learned to chop wood for the fire. To do our laundry, I hauled hot water to an old wringer washer that sat outside.

We lived in the trailer for about three months, then moved into town near an old mill, where I had gotten a job grading and bundling cedar roofing shakes. It was tough work that at the end of each day left my hands swollen from the cedar slivers that made their way through my gloves.

We lived in the small town of four hundred people for about five years, but were never really accepted into the community. Still, the kids and I tried hard to make it work. We cleared the land next to our home and created a baseball diamond. We always encouraged visitors and, despite being impoverished, always offered treats for those who visited. My son Jim even started a club called the Peacemakers, hoping to make friends with other youths.

However, after five years, I had grown tired of incident after incident of cruelty. We were repeatedly taunted not only as the "family who set their house on fire" but also as "goody two shoes," because we went to church. Our "better life" remained an elusive dream.

So, I decided to move my family from Washington state to Michigan, where my sister lived with her husband and two daughters, hoping to find our better life there.

We had few possessions, but we sold most of them to buy bus tickets and packed about sixteen boxes with personal items we wanted to keep. I made phone calls and lined up a rental house before we left. When we changed buses in Chicago, however, I called my sister and found out the people had decided they didn't want to rent to a single parent with so many children. So there we were again, with no place to stay and our new beginning slipping out of our hands before we even got to town.

We stayed with my sister's family in their small, two-bedroom condo until the owners of the condominium complex said the "visit" had extended beyond the allowed time. I wanted more than anything to have our own place, to work, and to lead a normal life. I again reached out to the state for help, and the public assistance department offered to help finance getting me into a place, but I was in for a huge shock. The welfare officials told me I had until 5:00 that evening to find a place or they would take my children from me. At 4:45, I reached an organization that helped people in my position. They spoke with the welfare office and put us in a motel for the night.

The next day we met with an attorney, who then contacted the state agency to arrange for emergency funds and to drop the threat to take my children. The first person he talked with refused to budge. He spoke to someone of higher authority, then to someone of even higher authority, and finally to someone very high up in the chain of command. The lawyer told the state agency he would call television and radio stations as well as newspapers and hold a press conference about what was happening. The agency backed down; we got the funds; and through some very nice people, we ended up in a rental house.

Unfortunately, the house was in miserable shape. Sewage went directly under the house, which was filled with flies, and the stove and refrigerator didn't work properly. But I was grateful to have a roof over our heads.

I started looking for a small church for us to attend but couldn't find one. One day a bright blue piece of paper blew past me as I walked down the street. I picked it up. It was an invitation to attend a large inner-city church that had bus service. I called to see whether they would pick up people in the area where we lived. They did, and I couldn't wait to attend church again, even if it was a large church.

The church was our new beginning. The parishioners were so warm and loving. I again became very active in the church, working there part-time and helping to start a day-care center. My son Jeff also worked at the nursery, where the children called him "Uncle Jeff."

A very remarkable man, a deacon in the church, bought a beautiful home just so I could rent it. We lived about a mile from a state mental hospital, and sometimes one of the patients stayed in our home too. Two of my children, David and Lisa, and I began a nursing home ministry. Once a week, we visited a local nursing home, where we read to the patients, prayed with them, and brought them little things like special slippers, stationery, or pretty pens.

Years of living with domestic violence and in a town that thought I was a criminal had destroyed my self-esteem. For a long while, I felt unworthy of receiving love. In our new town and new church, I was capable of giving and receiving love again.

Under God's plan all things work together for good. We finally found our new beginning, just a bit later than we planned.

—SUSAN STEVENS

*Various circumstances brought Susan and her family back to Washington, where she worked for the county, visiting the elderly and disabled in their homes. She then worked in a sewing factory for four years before returning to school. Today, she works in management for a human resources company. All seven of her children have grown into tender-hearted, caring, compassionate adults.*

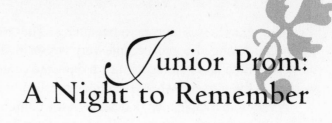

# Junior Prom:
# A Night to Remember

Dear Mr. and Mrs. Jones,

You don't know me, and I have never met your daughter. However, I wanted to tell you about an event that occurred recently and to express my appreciation to her and you.

Your daughter Brittany's act of kindness made what could have been a disastrous evening a memorable one for my son, Jonathan. I have enclosed a picture as well as his story.

For months, Jonathan had looked forward to his junior prom night and talked about it constantly. Because he didn't have a date but desperately wanted to attend, he arranged to go with a friend—a senior. They always planned to have a picture taken together and to go to a restaurant for dinner after the prom. She would then drive Jonathan home.

Her plans changed, but she didn't inform Jonathan. The "friend" left the prom quietly without telling Jonathan—leaving him with no transportation, no one to go out to eat with, and most important (to him), no one to have his picture taken with.

At that point, Jonathan asked Brittany (and her date) if she would have her picture taken with him. God bless her for saying yes! By the expression on his face in the photograph, no one would guess the letdown he had just experienced. When I picked him up at Robinson Auditorium at 10 P.M., he was the last student to leave. As I choked back those mother's tears, the first thing he said to me was, "Mom, I had so much fun, and guess what?! Brittany Jones had her picture taken with me."

What makes this story unique, Mr. and Mrs. Jones, is that Jonathan has a mild form of cerebral palsy due to complications caused by premature birth.

Professionals doubt he will ever drive a car. He has never experienced the excitement of a first date. Although he is active in a local church youth group, he doesn't frequent movies, malls, or restaurants, surrounded by friends. School is very important to him. He is self-motivated to study, likes attending school functions, and is usually content to sit on the side and watch others.

With his junior prom, he took a risk. Although his carefully orchestrated evening didn't turn out as planned, Brittany's sensitivity saved the day. He cherishes the pictures. The eight-by-ten photo hangs on the wall just inside his room.

I wanted you to have this picture and one more reason to be proud of your daughter. Brittany is truly a lovely young woman both inside and out.

—BRENDA K. CAMPBELL

*Jonathan is in his third year of college. He has found his niche in the performing arts and has appeared in plays at a local community theater. Between semesters, he volunteers at the YMCA and the Arkansas Repertory Theatre.*

# Carrier Pigeon

My parents divorced when I was about ten years old. It was an unhappy marriage, so it was a blessing to have the fighting end. My two brothers and I stayed with my mom. We didn't see much of my father after the divorce.

Although I recall little about the time spent with my dad during my first ten years, one thing stands out in my memory. I remember we raised homing pigeons together. He even gave me one of my very own. Her name was Little Red.

On weekends, we would load up the car with the pigeons in their cages and drive a great distance from home. When we were far enough away, Dad would pull the car over to the side of the road. He'd take each pigeon out of its cage, and wrapping both of his hands around its body, he would give the bird a great big toss into the air. We would watch them circle overhead and fly away. Then we'd climb back into the car and drive to a nearby store to pick up some sodas before heading home.

Come evening, we would sit on the back steps of our house, sipping our sodas and scanning the horizon, waiting for each pigeon's successful return. It never ceased to amaze me how each bird would fly directly back to the safety of its pen. My dad and I would turn to one another and cheer over this miraculous feat.

Over the next thirty years, I barely kept in touch with my dad. Over the course of a year, I'd talk with him only two or three times and see him maybe once. It wasn't a great distance that separated us; it was emotions. We both had a hard time expressing our love for one another. Ironically, although the pigeons we let go always made it home, once he left home, I found it hard to feel close to my father.

I once received a greeting card from him in the mail. It said he wished we had been the kind of family that lived in the same small town and spent evenings sitting out on the porch, sipping lemonade together and watching life go by. It was signed simply, "Love, Dad." I cried.

Not long ago, I got a call from dad. He had been sick for several months, and I had made and sent him a "hurry up and get well" card. He had phoned to tell me it was not to be; he had been diagnosed with lung cancer and given three to four months to live. I cried for hours that night over the time we'd lost and the time to come that we'd never have.

Dad lived for two months after that fateful call. We did get the chance to say our good-byes, for which I will always be grateful. I am also thankful he did not have to linger in pain for very long.

At Dad's memorial service, I received a very special gift. As I sat inside the church, listening to the beautiful hymns my father had selected, something flew in and perched on the altar: a pigeon. I knew it was my dad, sending a miraculous message directly to me—letting me know he'd made it safely home.

—WANDA MITCHELL

*Wanda Mitchell is a wife, mother, and grandmother residing in Alta Loma, California. She is a travel agent and librarian. Her hobbies include writing, crafting, and spending time with her family. She loves movies, music, sunsets, and traveling on cruise ships. Her prescription for life— enjoy it.*

# $\mathscr{L}$esson in Humility

I FELT A BIT NERVOUS THAT MORNING AS I GOT READY TO MEET MY SON at the superior court building. I knew I would soon have to face some good people who happened to hold a different opinion of justice than I did. I was contemplating what I would say or do if approached by one of these people, when the telephone rang.

My son, Jeff, was on the other end, asking, "How ready are you?"

I explained I had my hair in heat curlers and was in the process of getting dressed. He suggested I drive to his house and we take one vehicle to the courthouse. I agreed and told him I would meet him in about twenty minutes.

I finished getting ready, which took a little longer than I had planned. So, I quickly headed for the door, grabbing my purse and car keys along the way.

I live on the third floor of a fairly good size apartment complex. The stairways are open to the outside, as are the balcony-like walkways lined with the doors to apartments on each floor. The parking lot for the complex lies approximately fifteen feet from the bottom of the stairway. I had parked my car on the far side of the parking lot.

Leaving my apartment, I walked down the three flights of stairs and across the parking lot, unlocked the door to my car, and got in.

After starting the car, I noticed I was getting low on gas, but decided to go to my son's house and get the gas later. I am so glad I made that choice.

As I drove, my mind was on the music coming from my car radio and the possibilities of what could happen in court. About halfway to Jeff's house I realized I had forgotten something very important and gasped, "Oh, no!" Disbelief overcame me, followed closely by panic, with another very loud, "Oh No!" thrown in every few seconds. Let me tell you, going down the road at forty miles per hour is not the time to discover your memory is not what it was.

I turned the car around and headed for home. Parking the car directly in front of the stairway, I noticed some people walk by as I turned off my car, reached for my purse, and prepared to go back upstairs. Just then, a car pulled up next to me. A woman got out and walked toward the stairs.

I was thinking, "Go to the first floor; go to the first floor." She took the stairway to the top floor—my floor.

I got out of my car and started for the stairway. As I rounded the corner after the last flight of stairs, I came face to face with the woman I had watched go upstairs earlier. She smiled; I smiled. Then

I nonchalantly walked to my door, opened it, entered the apartment, locked the door, and called my son.

"Where are you?" he asked.

"I'm at home," I answered, "I forgot something and had to come back here to get it."

"What did you forget?" he asked.

I told him, and we both roared with laughter. I had left the house wearing everything except my black dress pants. Somehow, I don't think black pantyhose would have been appropriate attire for the courthouse.

I learned I am not only capable of doing something very embarrassing but also that I have the ability to turn the situation around and see the humor in it. I wonder if God was laughing as he watched me learn my lesson in humility.

—SUSAN STEVENS

*After this incident, Susan's son offered to buy her a full-length mirror for the back of her front door. She declined, because she now thoroughly checks to make sure she isn't forgetting anything before leaving the house.*

# Winds of Kindness

THE HURRICANE FLOYD EVACUATION OF 1999 WAS ONE OF THE MOST horrible experiences of my adult life. Because of the danger posed by this hurricane, possibly the worst in U.S. history, the authorities issued a mandatory order to evacuate our neighborhood and head inland.

An estimated 750 thousand automobiles, trucks, boats, motor homes, and campers lined every street, road, and highway, heading West out of harm's way. Floyd's 178-mile-per-hour winds of death roared at our backs, threatening to suck up and destroy everything we had worked so hard to accomplish and held dear to our hearts.

We had packed my wife, son, daughter-in-law, a friend, six dogs, three cats, some necessities, and myself into three small automobiles. As we traveled along Highway 82 from our home in Brunswick, Georgia, to Waycross, about twenty-five miles away, none of us realized we would encounter an even greater force of nature an hour down the road.

Traffic was so backed up we never traveled more than six miles per hour or moved forward more than 500 feet without having to stop. I turned on the C.B. radio to see whether there was an accident ahead.

I noticed a women and her friend stranded on the side of the road next to a car with its hood raised. The car had overheated, and passersby were jumping from their cars to give the women gallons of their own drinking water. As we passed and dropped off another gallon of water, the woman started pouring water into her radiator. Suddenly, the boiling water spewed back into her face, scalding the side of the head. Three or four strangers immediately jumped from their slow-moving cars and rushed to her assistance, offering towels and cooling off her radiator for her.

Another mile or so down the road, a trucker came on the C.B. radio to ask whether anyone could tell him where he could stop and get a soft drink. Because all the stores were either sold out of beverages or closed, he had nothing to drink. Someone responded, asking his location. He replied he was passing road marker nineteen. The other person told him to look on sign post twenty-one when he got to it. People instantly started honking their horns, which could be heard for miles. When we passed marker twenty-one, a cold, refreshing Mountain Dew sat on top of the marker.

Throughout the long exodus, people who ordinarily would be pushed to their limits under similar conditions were trying to help everyone they could. When we finally arrived in Waycross nine hours later (a drive that normally takes about thirty-five minutes), we had nowhere to go. All the motels in three states were full. We slept in our automobiles with the animals. It was one of the most restless nights I've ever encountered, but we made the best of it.

At about 6:00 the next morning, we got out of the cars and just stood around with thousands of other stranded people. It was cold and cloudy, and the wind was blowing about forty-five miles per hour. The local electric company came by, asking if we needed any help finding a shelter. However, the shelters didn't allow animals, and we weren't about to leave our pets, even if it meant passing up warmth and hot food. No restaurants within fifty miles were open. All the stores in the area were sold out of essentials, including bread.

Several hours later, an African–American woman stopped where we were huddled. She said, "I know you don't know me from Adam, but I'd like to invite you to my home for a hot shower and to clean up, if you wish." I almost fell over! I couldn't believe that in the midst of all that chaos this wonderful woman, Vera Finney, was driving around inviting total strangers into her home. (Why would an African–American woman stop to offer kindness to a large group of poorly dressed, tired white people when hundreds of other African–Americans were also standing around? I had lived for so long in an area of the country still dealing with racial tensions, this moved me even more. Could it be this woman's heart was color-blind?)

As we traveled to Ms. Finney's home, she talked about her new WebTV and how proud she was of it. Before leaving her house that day, my son and I, both WebTV wizards, packed her unit with search engines, folders, web sites, and as much stuff as we could squeeze in. We even signed her up as a new Heartwarmers4u member!

When the authorities gave the all-clear, we headed back to our warm, sweet home. I will never forget pulling off the freeway and seeing my home town as if it was a ghost town—not a car, human, or animal in sight. It was an unpleasant and dangerous experience I wish never to repeat.

However, not even the foul winds of a deadly hurricane could diminish the determination, fortitude, or compassion of the wonderful people who make this world as great as it is. When we ran from Floyd's fury, we found ahead of us a much more powerful force—the strong, but sweet, winds of kindness, friendship, courtesy, and love.

—Roger Dean Kiser, Sr.

*Roger and his wife, Judy, returned home to find everything safe and sound. Four days later, they went back to Waycross to have dinner at the "best seafood restaurant" in the area with their new friend, Vera Finney. Roger and Judy expect the friendship they share with Vera to last the remainder of their lives. This special friendship places three more stones in the bridge that will one day bring people together as one.*

# The Power of Popcorn

I CREPT UP TO THE DOOR AND KNOCKED. I WAS SCARED—JUST A LITTLE— but far too excited to pay the fear much attention.

A gruff voice bellowed (just another part of the routine), "Who is it?"

Quietly, I whispered, "It's Nancy, Mr. Hoag."

"What do you want?" he yelled. (As if he didn't already know.) Mr. Hoag's large figure approached the door, while a smile spread across his face. A smile was all I needed! I felt instantly reassured and welcomed. In a matter of seconds, I led my gang of four or five neighborhood kids and two brothers through the house to the living room.

There it stood—the complete set-up: Two chairs faced each other on either side of the square, iron floor register. In the center of the register was perched a huge, yellow, enamel washbasin filled to the rim with fresh, hot popcorn.

The aroma filled the air and caused a magnetic attraction—kids and snacks, a natural combination. No smell on Earth surpassed Mr. Hoag's homegrown, fluffy, white, kernel popcorn. A stack of white paper bags sat nearby on a little wooden stool.

One by one, we took our turn sitting on the chair opposite this grand man, chatting with him while he filled our bag. He listened to each one of us with great interest. Whether we told him our troubles or victories, he listened intently, and our opinions and words mattered to him. He never made fun of us for what we told him. We knew this person valued us and felt us worthy of his attention.

When we had finished our popcorn, we each gave him a heartfelt thank you and a warm hug—even the boys, except for John and Joey, the older ones. Mr. Hoag acknowledged their "big-boy" status with a handshake.

On the couch at the other end of the living room, Mr. Hoag's beautiful wife grinned as she watched the parade. Although they had no children of their own, Mrs. Hoag, an English teacher at my school, and Mr. Hoag were child-friendly folks. They loved us, and we could feel it. Strengthened, we confidently ran off with treats in hand.

I'm not sure which we loved more . . . the popcorn or Mr. Hoag! Our self-esteem was restored nightly by an ornery, seventy-five-year-old teddy bear who knew the power of popcorn.

—NANCY E. QUARTARARO

*Nancy's path has taken her from careers as a junior high school foreign language teacher, mother, restaurateur, and now freelance writer. She currently shares her home with two children, ages twenty-two and twenty.*

# All Alone

I WAS SIX YEARS OLD WHEN I WET MY PANTS AT SCHOOL FOR THE FIRST TIME. Because the orphanage staff only permitted us to use the bathroom when they thought it was necessary, I was afraid to ask my first-grade teacher for permission to use the little boy's room.

I'd just sit at my desk, shaking my little legs back and forth, hoping I could hold it until the bell rang. That day in school, however, I wasn't so lucky, because my stomach hurt so badly. I tried to release just a little at a time, so I wouldn't start crying or embarrass myself in front of the entire class. But once it started coming out, I couldn't stop it, and the pain just got worse and worse.

Several of the boys sitting behind me started laughing loudly. Then the entire classroom, realizing what had happened, also started laughing at me. The teacher motioned for me to come up in front of the classroom. She handed me some newspaper and told me to get down on my hands and knees and wipe up the mess, which had run under several of the desks. I tried to laugh along with the other children but was so ashamed I didn't know what to do or say. I just got on my knees and wiped very slowly, hoping the bell would ring before I had to look any of the other kids in the face.

Finally, the bell rang, and the kids ran out for recess, calling me names as they went by my desk. The teacher stood over me, telling me I should be very ashamed of myself and when the class resumed I was to stand with my face in the corner for the remainder of the day.

After I had cleaned up after myself, I walked out to the hallway and just stood there, too embarrassed to go out in the school yard with the other children. When the school bell rang again, all the children started to file back into the classroom. I quickly ducked into the bathroom and hid in one of the stalls with my feet up on the toilet seat until everything became quiet.

Then I ran out of the bathroom, down the long hallway, and out of the school building. I knew the teacher would call the orphanage and I would receive the switch or a beating when I returned that afternoon. So I decided to run away and never come back.

As I walked through different neighborhoods, I happened upon one house with the garage door open and a large rifle leaning against the wall. I walked up to the garage very slowly, looked around, then grabbed the rifle, and ran as fast as I could back down Spring Park Road to the school.

I crouched behind a large bush, where I could see the children moving around in my classroom. I opened the rifle to make sure it contained ammunition and found it fully loaded. At that point I wasn't sure what to do or where to go. I only knew I could never return to school or the orphanage and that I wanted to get even with everyone for laughing at me.

I stood for five minutes or so, listening to the sounds of the cars passing and the birds in the large bush singing. Slowly I raised the rifle, looked down the barrel, pointed the gun at the school window, and centered one child after another in its scope. Then, I directed my aim at several of the passing cars.

Finally, I made my decision, pointed the rifle, and placed my finger on the trigger, holding my breath. Then I closed my eyes tightly, and slowly pulled the trigger until the rifle jerked and fired with a bang, knocking me to the ground. I stood still for a moment, then let the rifle fall to the ground.

Feeling something wet on my skin, I took off my undershirt and wiped my face and eyes. As I picked myself up off the ground, a wave of nausea engulfed me. After a minute or so, I pulled myself together and slowly walked toward the large bush where I had been standing when I fired the weapon. I stared at all the blood in disbelief that I had done something so terrible.

I reached out and touched the blood with my finger. I dropped to my knees, fell onto my face and stomach in the dirt, and laid there crying. I looked upward at the beautiful blue sky and all the puffy white clouds, then I lowered my head back down into the dirt.

I stayed there for a long time, just looking at the most beautiful orange and black colors lying next to my head. The injured area, when I finally got up enough nerve to touch it, was still very warm. I'll never forget the limp, lifeless, broken neck and the warm, still body of the only thing I have ever killed in my whole life—a red-winged blackbird.

I returned the gun to the house from which I had taken it. I received one hell of a beating when I returned to the orphanage later that day—but it was a beating the six-year-old killer didn't mind taking. Until then, I had always thought nothing was worse than being an orphan with no one to love you. The next worse thing was having other children laugh at you because you had big ears or wet your pants. On that day, I discovered a feeling far worse—holding something warm and lifeless in the palm of my hand and knowing I had killed it.

As a grown man, I have sometimes looked back and wondered if that red-winged blackbird gave its own life to save the lives of others later.

—ROGER DEAN KISER, SR.

*Roger wrote this very difficult and secret story in the hope it might provide insight into the mind of an anguished child who could have made a very serious mistake at that time in his life.*

# Mom Is Love

WHILE GROWING UP, MY FAMILY CONSISTED OF ONLY MY MOTHER, WHOSE name is Kim, and me. We were as close as a mother and daughter could possibly be. My mom and I would go every weekend to a certain spot by this one lake, where we'd have a picnic and feed the ducks. I would dress up, turn a hairbrush into a microphone, and sing and dance for her just to see her beautiful smile. We spent all of our time together. My mom believed that God had sent me to her for a special reason, and I soon found out what that was.

A teacher once asked me what love was, and I told her, "My mom is love." Her smile was as bright as the sun; she was absolutely the most amazing person I have ever met.

Then one day my mom started complaining that her leg hurt her. The doctor said nothing was wrong, but it got to the point that she could not move without great pain. The doctor ran more tests and discovered she had a large tumor in her left leg. When I learned my mother had cancer, I didn't know what to think. I had never really heard of cancer and didn't understand the enormity of it. How could I, at age six, have imagined that this disease would take my mom away from me in only two years.

After her diagnosis, my life got turned upside down. Mom was sent to the best doctor in the state, who informed her she had to have surgery on her leg. My mom left our cozy little home in Port Allen, Louisiana, and traveled to Shands Hospital in Florida for the surgery. The doctors there performed the operation and said everything would be okay. But things were not okay. My mom's leg got infected and had to be amputated. During the three-month hospitalization in Florida, I saw her only once. During her absence, I felt lost and missed my mom.

When she finally came back and we were back together in our own home, life was great again. When she could drive again, we went shopping, and I pushed her around really fast in her wheelchair. We thought the "visitor" (cancer) was gone forever, but we were wrong.

The cancer returned. Mom was determined to beat it, and the doctors tried everything, but it spread to her lungs. She underwent more surgery and chemotherapy, which made her sick and lose her hair. Then she tried radiation treatments. I don't know how she did it, but she stayed strong and kept up her spirits. No matter how much pain she was in, she always did her best to put a bright smile on her face.

My mother hit rock bottom in March 1989. She was confined to bed, and the doctors could do no more for her. She knew she was dying and wanted to die at home. I didn't realize what was happening until I came home from school on Friday, March third. The whole family was in town, and I knew things were bad.

The last time I saw my mom, she was weak and pale. It took all of her strength for her to put her arms around me and hug me one last time. When I was leaving to go spend the night at my aunt's house, I looked at her and said, "I'll see you tomorrow, Mom." She looked at me with tears in her eyes and said, "Yes, Sweetheart, I will see you tomorrow. Brandi, don't ever forget how much I love you."

Even while dying, she was trying to protect me from the fact that I wouldn't see her again. The next day at noon my mom, my "love," let go and slipped away.

My mom taught me how to love, and what strength and courage are. She taught me how to find the good in all people and situations. I am twenty years old now and take strength from the fact that my mom is with me every day. She is still my best friend in life, and that will never change.

—BRANDI PATIN

*Brandi lives in Port Allen, Louisiana, in the same house she once shared with her mother. She works for a local day care center and is a volunteer firefighter in Port Allen.*

# Scottish Royalty

IN NOVEMBER 1961, WHEN I WAS SIXTEEN YEARS OLD, I COMPLETED MY Army basic training. I was stationed at Fort Gordon, Georgia, and from there was being sent to Fort Wainwright, in Fairbanks Alaska. I decided to take my leave in Jacksonville, Florida, where I had been raised in an orphanage.

As I arrived at the Trailways bus station in Jacksonville, I noted many unsavory types standing around on the street, which was not an unusual sight to me. I had seen it hundreds of times before, because I had lived on these streets for several years before a juvenile court order had placed me in the Army.

I guess I came back to the streets of Jacksonville to show everyone I had finally become somebody. I threw my duffel bag over my shoulder and started walking toward Forsythe Street.

Because I had no family, I decided to see whether I could find someone I knew from the times when I had lived on the street. Walking the two miles or so to Forsythe, I felt very uncomfortable, because Jacksonville was strictly a Navy town. The sailors gave me the evil eye as I strolled by them. Several sailors walking behind me started making comments about my uniform and how they could discard a certain "Army boy" if he didn't pick up his pace and get out of their way. I quickly turned into a coffee shop and ordered a soda.

After I was sure they had gone, I went back outside and was relieved to find they were nowhere in sight. I continued to walk toward town and stopped in an Army/Navy surplus store. About half an hour later, I emerged from the shop decorated with almost every medal known to mankind, not to mention my white spats and white pistol belt. I was one sharp-looking dude.

When I finally reached Forsythe Street and was walking by the Florida Theatre, I noticed the same three Navy guys giving another man, a dwarf, a hard time. They had pushed him off the sidewalk and were laughing at him. As I passed, I could see the little man had no legs and only some of his fingers, and his hands were callused from pushing himself around on a mechanics board. I had seen him many times before when I lived on the street, but I had never spoken to him, because he looked too scary to me. Unable to get up enough nerve to say anything to the sailors, I just walked on by.

The farther I got from them, the more I hurt inside. Finally, I could take it no more, and turned around and headed back. When I arrived, the sailors were already crossing the street. I noticed they had jammed a single dollar bill into the dwarf's mouth. I stood before him, looking down, not knowing what to say. I reached into the street to get his mechanics board and helped him get back on it. I told him I would buy him something to eat if he was hungry.

He replied he was hungry, so I took out my wallet and handed him a twenty-dollar bill. That was a lot of money for me, because I got only $68 a month in Army pay. As I turned to leave, he yelled at me to stop.

When I turned around, he asked if he could buy me dinner. So I walked and he rolled down the street to the Krystal hamburger stand, where we each ordered several hamburgers. We talked for about an hour. I told him I had no mother or father and had been raised in an orphanage on the Southside. He told me he didn't have parents either and had lived in an institution for about ten years. After we had eaten our meal, I paid for his hamburgers, so he could save his $20.

He asked me to wait while he went to get something important.

He finally returned about thirty minutes later, handed me a large envelope, and asked me not to open it until he was gone. I shook his deformed hand good-bye and then watched as he rolled himself back down the street toward the Florida Theatre. I folded the envelope, stuck it in my back pocket, and left the restaurant.

As I stepped out into the street, the same three burly-looking sailors immediately started shoving me around and finally pushed me against the plate-glass window. Several military policemen drove up and asked what was going on, and the three sailors just walked away laughing. The MPs got out of their vehicle, walked around me several times, and then one of them asked me, "Just what damn service are you in?"

"The French Foreign Legion," yelled one of the three sailors. Knowing I couldn't possibly have earned all those medals as a private first class, they laughed as they strutted off. The MPs handcuffed me for being out of uniform and took me to the Naval Air Station at Mayport to run a check on my military identification.

Several hours later, the MPs told me my leave had been canceled for being out of proper military uniform. They immediately took me to the Jacksonville International Airport and placed me aboard a flight to Fort Wainwright, Alaska, my ordered destination anyway.

A little while into the flight, I remembered the envelope the dwarf had given me. When I pulled it out and opened it, I found ten $100 bills, a note, and a page from a magazine. The note read, "I said I would take you out to dinner." The dirty, old, wrinkled magazine page featured a large picture of a man and a woman, standing next to a fancy, six-horse drawn carriage with a castle rising behind them. The headline read, "Scottish Royalty Dies, Deformed Infant Found and Placed in Institution."

At the bottom of the magazine page was handwritten, "A large steak would be nice. That's what I eat every day, my friend."

—ROGER DEAN KISER, SR.

*As badly as Roger was treated as a child in the orphanage, he has always tried to remember that others, even royalty, have also known the pain and sorrow of being pushed aside and unloved.*

# Never Give Up Hope

I SAT IN THE GROUP THERAPY ROOM OF THE COUNTY DRUG AND ALCOHOL treatment center, waiting to see what the therapist would say about the story of my life I had just finished telling.

"Dawn," he said, "Your life has been a tragedy, but you don't have to continue to live like this. There is a way out."

Life hadn't been easy for me from the time I was four years old. That was the year my baby sister was born. It was also the year I was molested by a family friend. Afterward, I started acting out and became a difficult child to deal with. No one knew why I had changed from a sweet four-year-old to a raging preschooler, and folks knew less about abuse than they do now. My rage continued through grammar school, where I spent the fourth grade in the hallway, and on into junior high, where I spent considerable time in the principal's office.

When I was eleven, I asked my mom to divorce my dad, an emotionally and physically abusive person. She did, and life went from bad to worse. Dad got custody, even after I testified against him in court.

We spent Sundays with Mama; she picked us up after church. We lived with Daddy during the week.

When I was twelve, my dad remarried, and his new wife brought her two daughters into our family. They were good kids, which made me look even worse! At fourteen, my dad's job transferred him from the only hometown I'd known to a sleepy little town in Alabama—700 miles away from my mom.

All of these events just fueled my rage. I got involved with the wrong folks and spent too much time with adults who had no business with teenagers. I started drinking beer, and soon I was on my way to some pretty rough stuff.

One night a friend and I sneaked out and went with her boyfriend to a nearby city to attend a party given by some college guys. Goodness knows how much Southern Comfort I drank that night. I can tell you I never drank it again! A few days later I somehow knew I was pregnant. I didn't tell my parents until about five months later, when I could no longer deny it.

My folks gave me one option for my unborn child: adoption. They sent me to a nearby home for unwed mothers, and a few months later I gave birth to a beautiful little girl I named Heather. Two weeks later, I was forced to sign papers, relinquishing her forever. I took a nose-dive.

I felt incredible emotional pain, as if someone had shot me with a cannon and blown a hole in my gut. But I wasn't allowed to openly grieve for my lost child. So, the hole got bigger, and I did anything to ease the pain and just forget. I drank whatever was put in front of me and took any drugs available to me. I overdosed several times, but somehow still lived.

At seventeen, I left home and over the next twenty years continued to go further and further down—lower than I thought any human being could go. In 1990, when I was thirty-four years old, I got involved with Rick, a good-looking guy who had been in and out of prison most of his life and was major trouble. He demanded I prove my love for him by getting involved in the crimes he committed to support himself. I added thief to my long list of sins, reaching a new low.

Then Rick got caught. The next day, for some weird reason, I returned to the scene of the crime, a local park. A park ranger recognized me as the person who had been with Rick the previous day, and he stopped my car. The person we had robbed the previous day was a doctor, and the police found his prescription pad under the seat of my car, tying me to the crime.

Jail was a horrible place! I had reached the bottom of the barrel. One day I sat down and wrote my mother, telling her to forget she had a daughter. In my eyes, I was scum, the lowest of the low. After three weeks, a friend bailed me out, and I went to stay with some friends. I knew my life was screwed up, and I wasn't sure there was any hope for me. I spent the next five or six years trying to clear the cobwebs out of my head, before I finally understood that the world was not going to change for me. I had to change, and the only way that was going to work was if I got into action.

I decided that, to fix my life, I had no choice: I wanted to find my daughter. I had been watching reunion shows on television for years, sobbing at every show. I hired private investigators and adoption search consultants, made phone calls, and wrote letters, searching in vain for my daughter. Five years later, I still had no clue where she was.

Then one day I was driving down the interstate when a voice spoke to me: "Dawn, it's time. Hire the best searcher in the country. You have the money in your 401K." I went home and talked it over with my husband, a wonderful man who I was lucky enough to have married a year and half earlier. With his blessing, I did hire the top, most expensive searcher in the United States. Three weeks later, she called me with my daughter's name, address, phone number, and parents' names. I held in my hand what I'd waited twenty-six years for.

A calm came over me. I reached out, picked up the phone, and dialed her number. When she answered, I said, "Hi, you don't know me, but I think I may know you. Is your date of birth July 26, 1972, and are you adopted? I think I may be your birth mother."

We talked for about forty-five minutes. At the end of the conversation, I was sure she was mine. I felt a joy like I'd never felt before. Later we confirmed that, yes, she was my Heather.

Life isn't perfect, I don't guess it will ever be, but some days I'm so grateful, tears stream from my eyes. Life is wonderful! I have my child, a loving husband, a home, a good job, and a church that considers me an important part of things—the list of blessings goes on and on! For all those years, I raged against God, blaming Him for my losses and all my pain. All along, He was just waiting for me to get clear enough to hear Him speak to me and to understand what He needed from me.

—DAWN ADAMS

*Dawn currently works as a senior administrative assistant for a major airline. She participates in adoption search and reunion and adoption reform. She visits with Heather on a regular basis, and Heather also has met her grandmother, aunt, and some of her cousins! Heather is a music teacher in a small-town middle school, using a talent that came from her birth mother, Dawn.*

*Now, here's something else that is truly amazing: When Dawn found Heather, her daughter was living by the name her adoptive parents had given her. When she was a child, she received a doll that came with an adoption decree. She named the doll Heather, having no idea her birth mom had named her Heather.*

# $\mathcal{W}$atching Over You

I WAS A SINGLE PARENT, RAISING A THIRTEEN-YEAR-OLD SON ALONE. MY son's father and I had divorced eleven years earlier.

My son, Michael, had decided to take up skiing at the nearby ski hill in Riverview, Michigan. One evening, I took him and his friend Joe to ski. Aware of the many troubled teens these days, I was always very careful about where they went and who would be there. It was a nice community ski facility, with an area for food and drinks in the upper loft.

I told the boys I'd watch them ski for a while (even though, in the evening with the lights on the hill, you could rarely tell any of them apart as they skied down). Most parents dropped off their kids and came back hours later. Before I could feel comfortable about leaving, however, I had to make sure they were safe and having a good time.

For several hours, I stood watching each little figure go up in the ski lift and then slowly ski downward. The boys came in a couple of times for some food and hot chocolate. They laughed and shared their triumphs and defeats of the hill, warmed up, and went off again.

After nearly four hours had gone by, I found myself standing in the window, feeling a bit lonely, sorry for myself, tired, and weepy. Thoughts of how my ex-husband was probably out having a great time with no responsibilities to tie him down started creeping into my head. How great it would be to be able to go clothes shopping or have some fun, something just for me for a change.

Suddenly, a voice broke through my self-pitying mood.

A young gentleman whom I had never met said "Hi, excuse me, but I noticed you've been standing there for hours watching your kids ski. Is that right?"

I responded, rather taken aback, "Yes, I have."

He replied, "Well, I just wanted to tell you, if more parents in the world were like you, this would be a better place to be." Then he pushed open the door and left, as suddenly as he had come.

My mood lifted, and a smile came to my face. I had often quoted a passage from the Bible: "Don't forget to entertain strangers, for by in so doing some have entertained angels unaware." When the stranger had spoken, a very strange but comfortable feeling engulfed me. I felt God had sent this man, this angel, to remind me of what was really important in this life. I knew in my heart there was nowhere else I'd rather be and nothing else I'd rather be doing at that moment.

—LINDA FERRIS

*Linda's son, Michael, is now twenty, graduated from high school, working full time, and in a relationship with a lovely girlfriend. Linda sometimes misses the days of standing and watching him skiing down the hill. Linda went to nursing school to become a registered nurse and now works as an ob-gyn nurse at a local hospital.*

# The Bicycles

ON THE MORNING OF THE FIRST DAY OF THE 1999 ROSH HASHANA, THE
Jewish New Year, I awoke with a familiar feeling I've had for several
years during my marriage to my husband, Stephen. It was a feeling of
loneliness. I am in a mixed marriage. We somehow manage our religious differences throughout the year, but they become particularly
difficult for me to handle during the Jewish High Holidays.

We are not an interfaith couple; we are both Jewish. Yet, Stephen and
I travel very different religious paths. My husband feels most comfortable
praying in an Orthodox Synagogue; he is a kosher, commandment-
abiding, traditional, Hebrew-literate Jew. His idea of heaven on the High
Holidays is spending full days in synagogue. I am a Reform Jew who
abhors going to synagogue, no longer sure of my own Jewish path or to
which Jewish community I belong.

I do not join my husband in synagogue. The Orthodox manner of
prayer seems alienating and foreign to me. Tradition prohibits me from
sitting next to him without a *mehitza*—the wall that allows traditional

Jewish men to pray without the distraction of the beauty of women around them. I do not understand Hebrew, and after only moments of squirming in my seat in the "ladies section," I want to go home.

I don't really want to be home alone either. That's why I feel lonely on Rosh Hashana, when most of the world's Jews attend synagogue or gather with other Jews. Even Jews who pay little attention to their Judaism throughout the year somehow find their way to a synagogue or Jewish community for Rosh Hashana and Yom Kippur. I could attend another synagogue in town or out of town without my husband, but I choose not to. I am not a member of another Jewish community, and sitting alone in a synagogue filled to capacity with Jews whom I do not know would not relieve my loneliness.

This year, an exchange student from Germany, Hendrik, joined us for the school year. He needed a bicycle but didn't have the money to purchase a new one. We devised a plan to make the rounds of yard sales until we found an acceptable bike for Hendrik. We tried on several occasions to find the perfect bicycle, but Hendrik is a tall boy, and the bicycles we found were all too small. Yard-sale season was nearing its end.

At 7:30 a.m. the morning of Rosh Hashana, Stephen headed off to worship services, dressed in his finest garb. As he started his walk (he doesn't drive on the holidays), I piled the three babies and Hendrik into the car. I could see the judgment in Stephen's eyes as we headed down the street. We were going yard-sale shopping for a bicycle for Hendrik—on the Jewish Sabbath and the first day of Rosh Hashana. Strong Jewish commandments forbade me from such secular activities. I could probably do nothing more inappropriate that day, other than eating bacon with eggs before we left. We keep a kosher home, so I at least refrained from that corruption.

I did not leave easily on our journey. Angst, guilt, remorse, and sadness filled me. Truthfully, I wanted to belong somewhere else: a community filled with Jews who would welcome me and miss me when I didn't attend worship services. I wanted my heart to fill with prayer. I wanted to clear my conscience by being a "good Jew" who attended synagogue and refrained from secular activities on this most important Jewish holiday. I wanted to take the holiday seriously, but I felt lost. I did not know how.

Shoving away my loneliness and confusion, I headed toward an address I had seen in the paper under the banner, "Huge Development Yard Sale!" Five minutes later I noticed a house on the road with two bicycles parked at the entrance to the driveway. As we drove past, a gentleman placed a sign on the bicycles that read "free."

The man was not holding a yard sale. Only the bicycles sat in his driveway. I thought that there must be a catch—perhaps they hadn't worked in years. I stopped the car and got out to converse with him.

"Excuse me, are those bicycles really free?" I asked.

"Yes," he replied. "My wife and I don't use them anymore, so we are giving them away."

"Is there anything wrong with them?" I queried.

"Nope," he reassured me, "they ride just fine."

Hendrik test drove one of the bicycles, and it was a perfect fit. I hadn't been on a bicycle since childhood, but since it was free, I told the gentleman we'd take both of them.

We couldn't fit the bicycles in my car. The stranger offered to throw them into his pickup truck. Then he followed us home, depositing our new bicycles in our driveway and driving off for his day.

I do not know who that angel was or why he chose to give away two perfectly fine bicycles. But I know this: I felt God reach out to me in my loneliness. Despite all of my angst about shopping on the Sabbath and on Rosh Hashana, He supplied me with two free bicycles, so I wouldn't have to buy them at all. Instead of judging me, the way I was judging myself, he gave me a miracle. The sign on the bicycles read "free," but they could have read "God."

I had convinced myself that God was in synagogue with all the "serious" Jews. I thought perhaps He had forgotten me, because I was being disrespectful to Him. But he was right near me, sitting on a bicycle.

I haven't ridden a bicycle in years, but perhaps I'll learn how to ride this one.

—AZRIELA JAFFE

*Azriela wrote the book,* Two Jews Can Still Be a Mixed Marriage, Reconciling the Religious Differences in Your Jewish Marriage *to help other Jewish couples resolve the religious differences that arise in their daily lives together. Next year she's not going shopping on Rosh Hashana.*

# Quiet Love

I'M SURE ALMOST EVERYONE HAS HEARD OF "TOUGH LOVE." BUT I WONDER how many people have heard of "quiet love." Quiet love was demonstrated to me by two wonderful people, my grandparents, lovingly known as Mama and Papa.

Mama was very short and as round as she was tall; Papa was a tall man who to me seemed to be nothing but legs. Papa talked very little, and when he did, he talked so low you could hardly hear him.

Papa and Mama had eleven children; nine grew to adulthood. I asked Papa one time how many grandchildren and great-grandchildren he had, and he answered, "Enough to love, too many to count."

I remember summer dinners under the shade trees, and Christmas Eves with so many people in the house you couldn't move or breathe for the heat. But what I remember the most was the quietness of the two. I loved to go over to their house at night and sit a spell after my mother and I finished supper. I think back on that time and wonder why I liked to go, because that is what we did—sit. With Papa in his chair and Mama in her rocker, we would sit. No one said much of anything. But I loved it. Why?

One day I asked Mama how they managed never to fuss. Mama told me that when they were "young'uns" and married only a short while, Papa came in from the field in a bad way. He snapped at her and then felt bad about doing it.

So he told her, "Mama, from now on when I have had a bad day, I will come in with my hat on backwards and that way you will know to walk gently."

Mama said, "When I have had a tiring day, I will put my apron on backwards, and you will know to do the same."

I remember Papa grinned and said, "That's why Omie's dress tail is always clean."

I saw their quiet love demonstrated many times. Papa had been in a car accident that left him with a broken neck. Mama made the 50-mile trip every day and stayed by his side from early morning until night. They did very little talking, but I believe Mama did much praying.

The quiet love came through. In their winter years, Papa had rheumatoid arthritis and for the last five years of his life was in a wheelchair. Mama stayed by his side and tended to him at times like he was a baby.

Then one night Mama sat down in her rocker, and her head dropped over. Papa rolled his wheelchair over to her and tried to arouse her. He called one of his daughters, and the ambulance came to take Mama away while Papa watched. He went to the hospital and stayed by her side as much as he could and spent the rest of his time in the intensive care unit's waiting room. Mama died a few days later. Papa continued to sit in his chair in the same place. The quiet love was still there. You could feel it every time you went into the room.

Papa reunited with Mama two years later.

My grandparents' love for each other brought great peace to me while they lived, and it continues to do so. I believe they are together in heaven now, peacefully sitting, because no words are necessary in their quiet love.

—MAXINE WRIGHT

*Maxine Wright lives in Bremen, Georgia, with her husband of thirty-four years. She works at an architectural firm and spends as much time as possible with her two daughters, two sons-in-law, and four grandchildren.*

# $\mathscr{A}$ Two-Wheeler

WHEN I WAS ELEVEN YEARS OLD, MY DAD, A PROFESSIONAL SINGER, WAS offered a good singing job in Miami Beach, Florida. My Mom, Dad, and I (we called ourselves the three bears) packed up and moved from Atlantic City, New Jersey, to Florida. As things turned out, the job fell through, and Daddy took various jobs to make ends meet.

It was nearing Christmas, and with all my heart I longed for a two-wheel bicycle—any color would do. It was in the back of my mind all the time. However, I didn't talk about it much, because I knew Mom and Dad were struggling with money. My parents had always sacrificed and done everything they could to make sure every Christmas was special for me.

I went to bed that Christmas Eve with visions of a two-wheel bicycle I knew I couldn't have. Little did I know that, while I slept, my father took a long bus ride from Miami Beach to Miami city to buy a bicycle from someone there. He then rode the bicycle back from Miami city—over the bridge, across the highways, and through all the traffic—back to our little apartment in Miami Beach.

On Christmas morning, the first thing to greet my half-opened eyes was a bright red, two-wheel bicycle! I was the happiest little girl alive and thought I must have the most wonderful Dad in the whole world.

I was right. I did. He gave me more than a red bicycle that Christmas—he gave me his love. Now that I am older and have my own family, I truly realize and treasure what a totally remarkable and unselfish person my Dad was. God bless him.

—JOYCE CAROL STOBBE

*Many years have passed since Joyce's two-wheeler experience. Yet, somewhere in the back of her mind, she searched for a man with qualities similar to her father's. After traversing many mountains and valleys, she is now married to a generous, caring man. She has an adult son as well as numerous stepchildren, stepgrandchildren, and step-great-grandchildren, none of which live at home with Joyce and her husband. Her large family is quite a bonus for the little girl who grew up as an only child, looking forward to her first two-wheel bicycle.*

# "Red"

FOR AN ELEVEN-YEAR-OLD AWAY FROM HOME FOR THE FIRST TIME, UCLA Medical Center was a big, scary place. The sounds and smells seemed so foreign: white shoes squeaking on highly polished floors; the intercom paging people; strange buzzers sounding; and the faint odor of alcohol lurking in the hallways.

A young girl about my age with beautiful eyes and a bright smile occupied the bed next to me and closest to the window. I wondered how she could seem so happy in this strange place. She had gone through a glass sliding door, and bandages covered her stitches. Despite the pain I knew she must have been experiencing, she was a friendly and welcome companion.

During the late 1950s, doctors discovered a tumor in the bone marrow of my right ankle. My foot had discolored and swollen until it no longer resembled an ankle. I went to UCLA for treatment. One day while I was away from my hospital room undergoing a battery of tests, my roommate and companion was released and went home. Without her to take my mind off my fears, I withdrew, silently retreating into books or television.

A few days later a rather frail-looking, freckle-faced, red-haired boy named Richard peeked in and said, "Hi!" He hopped on the empty bed near the window and began to chat as if we were old friends. He talked about places he wanted to visit, favorite games, television shows, and how sick he was.

His eyes sparkled and, other than being very pale, he didn't seem sick to me. He loved to perform small skits and kept those of us in the children's ward laughing.

His father, too, came to visit us. A taller, older, and broader version of my friend, his father was just as funny as Richard. His kindness made you feel warm and comfortable around him. We all enjoyed his visits and the humor and laughter he brought with him.

Then the day came when my doctor told me I needed surgery. Gently, he told me there was a good chance he would have to amputate my leg. I remember crying in fear for hours that night. Because my mother had three small children at home to care for, she couldn't be with me, and I felt alone and scared. I had a difficult time falling asleep. When I finally fell asleep, it wasn't for long.

I awoke to find Richard's father asleep in the chair next to my bed. He woke up soon after I did and in a very gentle voice kept telling me it was going to be okay and that I just had to believe. He stayed for most of the night. I would sleep for a while and then wake up to see him still there. Sometimes he was asleep; other times, he smiled and comforted me.

Surgery went well, and I didn't lose my leg. However, I was in and out of surgeries, casts, and the hospital for the next two years. During the second year of my illness, Richard passed away from leukemia, but has lived on in my heart and memory.

His father became my hero then and in later years. During the time I knew Mr. Skelton and his son Richard, I only saw their courage, compassion, and tender hearts.

I saw the man who when "in character" made the children laugh and forget their illnesses. I also saw a very gentle man who, when not "in character," sat by the bed of a frightened, fatherless eleven-year-old girl.

Setting aside his own fears and sadness, "Red" Skelton, the clown who entertained millions during the early days of television, helped me face a scary situation with the hope it was going to be okay.

—SUSAN STEVENS

*Susan married at fifteen and had eight children, including twins, by the time she was twenty-two! She has been a single parent since her mid–twenties, and all her kids are now grown and doing well. She works as a manager for a human resource services company and enjoys her writing hobby.*

# Just Because

SEVERAL YEARS AGO I SPENT OVER A MONTH IN THE HOSPITAL. DURING my hospitalization, my coworkers covered my job, visited me, and sent me flowers and cards. They warmly welcomed me back when I returned and helped me while I re-acclimated. I decided I had to show my appreciation.

One day during lunch I visited my favorite florist and bought a beautiful flower arrangement she had in the cooler. I had it delivered to a coworker who had been extra caring, and signed the card "Just Because," with no name. I swore the florist to secrecy.

When the arrangement arrived, my coworker's face glowed. What a buzz went around the office that afternoon. Everyone was speculating about her secret admirer, and I went along with the excitement.

The next day during lunch, I picked another floral arrangement and had it delivered—"Just Because"—to one of my other coworkers who also had been very gracious. I had another "Just Because" bouquet delivered to still another caring coworker on the third day.

What a stir the mystery flowers created. My puzzled coworkers phoned the florist, inquiring into the identity of this mysterious admirer. The florist, being the sweetheart she is, revealed nothing.

A wonderful atmosphere filled the office. The whole department teamed up to solve the mystery. My colleagues made whoever received flowers the special person for the day, showering her with attention and admiration. With the warmth and excitement flowing through the department, I couldn't stop then.

I heard some of the guys saying, "Men don't like flowers—sure glad I didn't get any."

The next day, one of my male coworkers received a "Just Because" arrangement. His chest swelled with such pride in being part of the happening that the buttons almost burst from his shirt!

The florist also got caught up in the excitement. Every day she waited for me to come in and pick out the special arrangement for the next "Just Because" delivery. The delivery girl waited just as excitedly to make her next delivery. After lunch my coworkers waited for the receptionist's phone call to see who had received that day's "Just Because" arrangement.

Meanwhile, the gaiety, wonder, and camaraderie spread to other departments. The joy in my heart overflowed. Feeling happy and loved, people were working to their capacity and enjoying the whole "Just Because" experience. The event went on for over three weeks.

The final "Just Because" arrangement arrived at the end of a staff meeting. I wrote and distributed a special thank you to everyone in the department, revealing the identity of their secret "Just Because" admirer.

The love and good cheer continued in our department for quite some time. I will never forget the glow on the face of each "Just Because" person on their special day. Nothing will equal the fulfillment I received from simply returning kindness.

—CINDA WEISS

*Cinda Weiss and her husband have retired and moved to a farm in Edgerton, Wisconsin, where Cinda spends her time remodeling, gardening, and writing. The work associates she sent flowers to remain very dear friends. She still loves to send flowers and cards to her friends and loved ones for all occasions as well as "Just Because."*

# Please Send Me Autumn

MY WIFE AND I WED WHILE I WAS IN THE NAVY. JUST A FEW SHORT months before my last cruise, she started bugging me for a list of things to send in "care packages" while I was at sea. For some reason, I had a hard time with the list. After she reminded me (again) that I needed to get the list to her before I left, I wrote her a letter. I left it with her as she watched me walk down the pier toward my boat. It read:

My Love,

You've asked what you can send me while I'm on cruise—those things that I want but cannot get while on the ship thousands of miles away. The list was fairly easy to write. I suspect it won't be as easy to fill.

Please send me autumn. Fill a box with the special chill the evenings get foreboding the cold of winter—that Jack Frost nip. Add the colors of fall: the yellows, reds, and browns of leaves whose cycle of life has ended. Send me the sound fallen leaves make as you shuffle through ankle-deep blankets of them scattered across the yard. Be sure to wrap some of the fragrant smoke that spirals up from the pile as they burn. Package with it the yellow harvest moon caught in the naked branches of a tree that has begun its winter sleep.

Later, you can send me winter. Send me the first heavy snow-fall—the muted, magical silence that comes down across the land as the fat flakes pile up quickly. Don't forget the taste of snowflakes on my tongue or the dusting of snow caught in your hair like jewels. Send me a blanket of white under a full moon, when the land seems to glow.

Send me a snowman or, better yet, a snow family with a snow-daddy, a snow-mommy, and little snow children with button eyes, sticks for arms, and carrots for noses. Send me an evening in front of a fireplace with hopes and dreams in the flames. Send me some of your warmth, as we snuggle beneath the covers on a cold December night. Don't forget icicles, long sturdy ones and thin delicate ones.

The holidays, too, I'll want those. Send me Halloween with the little witches, ghosts, cowboys, and pirates. Carefully wrap for me the shy voices that whisper "trick or treat" from the little fairies joining in the ritual for the first time. Package them carefully with the louder, bolder cries of the more experienced trolls and Indians hidden safely behind disguises they are sure could fool even their parents. Send me the smell of freshly carved pumpkins with their funny or horrifying jack-o-lantern grins and snarls.

Capture for me some of the more grown-up magic that comes later that night, near the witching hour, after the little ones are tucked in their beds and the house is quiet, except maybe for a branch against the window. Even adults get an uneasy feeling that perhaps there are haunts and goblins about in the night.

Save for me the smells of roast turkey and dressing, homemade breads and pies. Send me the smells of Thanksgiving, as the food cooks all day and the table piles higher and higher. Send me that quiet sense of pride and accomplishment that rests briefly between setting the table and the feasting frenzy.

Send me a Christmas tree—not just any tree, but a live one felled by small hands assisted by a mom and dad. Send it with the fresh-cut smell and draped in sparkling lights and tinsel carelessly tossed here and there by young'uns trying to outdo each other. Send me a glass of eggnog, ever so gently spiked. Take your sips first and leave the prints from your lips on the glass for me to see and taste.

Send me the sleepless anticipation of the night before Christmas, when little angels try so hard to go to sleep, knowing in their hearts Santa won't come until they do. Share with me a glass of milk and a couple of chocolate chip cookies to help preserve the fleeting illusions of childhood. Send me the excited shouts as little ones get their first glimpses of the piles of gifts left by St. Nick. Send the crinkle and tear of wrapping paper and the oohs and aahs that punctuate each gift as it is exposed and shown around. Send me the hugs as everyone opens the gifts that were "just what I wanted!"

For the last day of the year, send me a quiet evening spent with you as we look forward to another year together, marveling at all we survived the year before.

Space out the packages, but send me all the changes of season, all the day-to-day worries and joys, all the holidays that I'll miss as I sit halfway around the world from you. Most of all, send me your thoughts and hopes, your dreams and wishes, and your smiles and tears.

Most of all, send me your love.

God Bless,

Ozzie

—DAVID E. OSBORNE

*David retired from the Navy in the spring of 1998 and now attends Southern Illinois University, where he majors in journalism. His wife is content in knowing that when she watches him leave these days, he's back in a few hours rather than a few months.*

# Contact Information

**The Red Mahogany Piano**
Joe Edwards
1521 E. Whiteside
Springfield, MO 65804
Phone: 417-889-4257

**My Little Brother**
Paul W. Kleinschmidt
4642 Utah, #4
San Diego, CA 92116
E-mail:
pkleinsc@hanoverdirect.com

**Nightly Friends**
Ern Grover
26 Webster St.
Springvale, ME 04083
Website:
www.ticktock.bizhosting.com/
home.htm
E-mail:
ern@ticktock.bizhosting.com

**Behind the Mirror**
Laura Reilly
8350 Boulevard East, Apt. 5H
North Bergen, NJ 07047
E-mail:
LKDOWREY@aol.com

**A Second Father**
Melissa Knapp
P.O. Box 89
Nelson, PA 16940
The Meanest Mother in the
World Site
Website:
www.members.tripod.com/
meanmother/
E-mail:
meanestmother@cheerful.com

**Just the Way You Are**
Susan Lingo Spence
3617 Northbrook Circle
Van Buren, AK 72956
E-mail: ARPoet@aol.com

**Elijah**
Azriela Jaffe
P.O. Box 209
Bausman, PA 17504
Phone: 717-872-1890
Website:
www.isquare.com/crlink.htm
E-mail: az@azriela.com

**Innocent Faith**
Rebecca O. Hayes
9238 East Palm Tree Dr.
Scottsdale, Arizona
85255–5544
E-mail: rolandhays@aol.com

**The Playhouse**
Patricia Fong
E-mail:
Patrisha_Howard@excite.com

**Forever in Her Debt**
Larry Harp
E-mail:
preacher81@earthlink.net

**Cat Angel**
Judy Guarino
288 East Main St., Unit #3
Branford, CT 06405

**Three Words**
Stephen J. Hopson
35820 Jefferson Ave., Ste. 206
Harrison Township, MI 48045
Fax: 734–629–0480
Website: www.sjhopson.com
E-mail: sjhopson@ibm.net

**Don't Let Life Pass You By**
Teresa Annklein Beaver
E-mail: PowRpac@aol.com

**Asleep at the Wheel**
Robin Nisius
1111 Schons St.
Evansdale, IA 50707
Phone: 319-232-5008 or
319-232-2720
E-mail: robin@kca.net

**Beautiful Eyebrows**
Robin Silverman
P.O. Box 13135
Grand Forks, ND 58208-3135
Phone: 701-787-0946
Website:
www.robinsilverman.com
E-mail:
creativisions@yahoo.com

**The Bathtub**
Michael T. Powers
1918 Liberty Ln.
Janesville, WI 53545–0918
Website: www.members.aol.com/
Thunder27/index.html
Email: Thunder27@aol.com

**Laddie McCrea**
Mike Kleiman
4045 Montrose Ct.
Orlando, FL 32812
E-mail: mike_kleiman@
compuserve.com

**Wubber Wooban**
Susan Fahncke
1325 North Highway 89, Ste. 315F
Farmington, UT 84025
Website:
www.fawnkey.com/susan.htm
E-mail: Susan@fawnkey.com

**Mother's Silver Candle
Sticks**
Liesel Shineberg
320 P. Street
Rock Springs, WY 82901
Phone/fax: 307-362-6457
E-mail: liesel@fiw.net

**Yard Sale**
Cheryl and Mike Norwood
321 McLain St.
Canton, GA 30114
E-mail: luvbirds@gateway.net

**Just Wanted to Talk**
Christina M. Abt
Crystal Hill Farm
9411 SandRock Rd.
Eden, NY 14057
Email: tre2tbl@gateway.net

**Awestruck Wonder**
Joe Edwards
1521 E. Whiteside
Springfield, MO 65804
Phone: 417–889–4257
E-mail: frogwilly@webtv.net

**Mystery Man**
Susan Stevens
6616 N. Addison St., #B 303
Spokane, WA 99208
E-mail: summr@msn.com

**The Face of God**
Tony Collins
1212 Fillmore
Wichita Falls, TX 76309
Website:
www.geocities.com/Heartland/
Estates/9892/
E-mail: Readcoll@aol.com

**Gratitude**
Liesel Shineberg
320 P. St.
Rock Springs, WY 82901
E-mail: liesel@fiw.net
Phone/fax: 307-362-6457

**In Dad We Trust**
Debbie Dobson
16609 Spring View Dr.
Lockport, IL 60441
Phone: 815-838-7020
E-mail: ddobson@lths.org

**The Rainbow**
Rose Gordon
50511 Galaxy Dr.
Granger, IN 46530
E-mail:
On_Wings@worldnet.att.net

**Heart Muscles**
Azriela Jaffe
P.O. Box 209
Bausman, PA 17504
Phone: 717-872-1890
Website:
www.isquare.com/crlink.htm
E-mail: az@azriela.com

**Who Am I?**
Betty E. Bergstrom
5419 SE Steele
Portland, OR 97206
E-mail:bettyberg@hotmail.com

**Gladly Give Everything**
David Sims
21612 Villa Pacifica Circle
Carson, CA 90745-1738
E-mail: Sims-usa@juno.com

**Josh and Beau**
Debbie A. Carter
7120 Wyoming NE,PMB5–109
Albuquerque, NM 87109
E-mail: dac082561@juno.com

**Kassidy**
Corrina Hyde
1501 N. 7th, Apt. 10
Durant, OK 74701
E-mail: crina_37@yahoo.com

**Transformations**
Lynne Daroff
E-mail: LBDaroff@aol.com

**She Lied**
Wanita Bates
South Florida Community
College
3077 Holiday Beach Dr.
Avon Park, FL 33825
E-mail: South Florida
Community College

**Christmas Angel**
Lynne Daroff
E-mail: LBDaroff@aol.com

**An Old Chipped Bowl**
Janet M. Hounsell
P.O. Box 374
Conway, NH 03818-0374
E-mail:
janeth@landmarknet.net

**When a Camper Goes "No Mail"**
Grace Witwer Housholder
The Funny Kids Project
816 Mott St.
Kendallville, IN 46755
Website: www.funnykids.com
E-mail:tghous@noble.cioe.com

**Broken Legs**
Roger Dean Kiser, Sr.
100 Northridge Dr.
Brunswick, GA 31525
Phone: 912-261-0048
Website: www.geocities.com/
athens/rhodes/3055/
E-mail:
trampolineone@webtv.net

**More than a Roll of Quarters**
John Kenneth King
1712 Turfland Ct.
Murfreesboro, TN 37127
E-mail: sriver@hotcom.net

**Sold It for Scrap**
Katherine Grimes
412 Moody Dr.
Valdosta, GA 31602
E-Mail:
kgrimes4@hotmail.com

**Typesetter's Apron**
Janet M. Hounsell
P.O. Box 374, Conway, NH
03818–0374
E-mail:
janeth@landmarknet.net

**Something About Harvey**
Kim Vorbau
2415 N. Old State Rd.
Delaware, OH 43015
Phone: 740–524–4402
E-mail:
Kim.Vorbau@dnr.state.oh.us

**Gino's Haircut**
Christina M. Abt
Crystal Hill Farm
9411 SandRock Rd.
Eden, NY 14057
Email: tre2tbl@gateway.net

**Still Waters**
David and Cindy Sims
21612 Villa Pacifica Circle
Carson, CA 90745-1738
E-mail: sims-usa@juno.com

**Last of the Flour**
Opal Martin Jayne
3137 Crescent Ave.
Marina, CA 93933

**Old-Fashioned Perfect Love**
Michael T. Powers
1918 Liberty Ln.
Janesville, WI 53545–0918
Website:
www.members.aol.com/
Thunder27/index/html
E-mail: Thunder27@aol.com

**A Tiny Miracle**
The author does not wish to be
contacted.

**A Perfect Little Number**
Timothy P. Henderson
485 Oneida St.
Lewiston, NY 14092
E-mail: Scatman50@aol.com

**Give Him All That You Have**
Anita Wise
E-Mail: Nita544349@aol.com

**My Guardian Angel, Kim**
Kathie M. Guidry
440 Avenue C
Port Allen, LA 70767
E-mail: Nannybug@webtv.net

**He Rescued Me**
Lisa Johnson Bartel
Mark, Lisa, Nora, Vic, Annie,
Eliza, Samantha, and Jacob
Bartel
Minnesota
E-mail:
javabean@computerpro.com

**Angels Along the Way**
Susan Stevens
6616 N. Addison St., #B 303
Spokane, WA 99208
Website:www.geocities.com/
Heartland/Park/4746
E-Mail:
Summr@email.msn.com

**Junior Prom: A Night to Remember**
Brenda Campbell
407 Calloway Ave.
Sherwood, AK 72120
E-mail: CampbellBrendaK@
exchange.uams.edu

**Carrier Pigeon**
Wanda Mitchell
8535 La Vine St.
Alta Loma, CA 91701
E-mail: TRAVEL980@aol.com

**Lesson in Humility**
Susan Stevens
6616 N. Addison St., #B 303
Spokane, WA 99208
E-mail: summr@msn.com

**Winds of Kindness**
Roger Dean Kiser, Sr.
100 Northridge Dr.
Brunswick, GA 31525
Phone: 912-261-0048
Website: www.geocities.com/
athens/rhodes/3055/
E-mail:
trampolineone@webtv.net

**The Power of Popcorn**
Nancy E. Quartararo
11 Chestnut St.
Akron, NY 14001
E-mail:
nancyq2@net.bluemoon.net

**All Alone**
Roger Dean Kiser, Sr.
100 Northridge Dr.
Brunswick, GA 31525
Phone: 912-261-0048
Website:www.geocities.com/
athens/rhodes/3055/
E-mail:
trampolineone@webtv.net

**Mom Is Love**
Brandi Patin
1590 Court St., Lot 35
Port Allen, LA 70767
E-mail: Brandisav@aol.com

**Scottish Royalty**
Roger Dean Kiser, Sr.
100 Northridge Dr.
Brunswick, GA 31525
Phone: 912-261-0048
Website: www.geocities.com/
athens/rhodes/3055/
E-mail:
trampolineone@webtv.net

**Never Give Up Hope**
Dawn Adams
4755 Campbellton Fairburn Rd.
Fairburn, GA 30213
E-mail:
adamsfam@rocketmail.com

**Watching Over You**
Linda Ferris
Lincoln Park, MI
E-mail: LAFRN10@aol.com

**The Bicycles**
Azriela Jaffe
P.O. Box 209
Bausman, PA 17504
Phone: 717-872-1890
Website:
www.isquare.com/crlink.htm
E-mail: az@azriela.com

**Quiet Love**
Maxine Wright
604 South Pecan St.
Bremen, GA 30110
Fax: 770-333-7902
E-mail: maxine@aroush.com

**A Two-Wheeler**
Joyce Carol Stobbe
P.O. Box 2806,
La Pine, OR 97739
(June–September)
P.O. Box 8614, Apache
Junction, AZ 85278
(October–May)
E-mail: Jcjoy2u@aol.com

**"Red"**
Susan Stevens
6616 N. Addison St., #B 303
Spokane, WA 99208
Website: www.geocities.com/
Heartland/Park/4746
E-Mail:
Summr@email.msn.com

**Just Because**
Cinda Weiss
8819 N. State Rd., #184
Edgerton, WI 53534
E-mail: Farm1ady@aol.com

**Please Send Me Autumn**
David E. Osborne
P.O. Box 111
De Soto, IL 62924
E-mail:
ozzie@brew-meister.com